T0209848

# JUST CALL ME
# DAD

## 13 Principles for Better Dads, Better Kids and a Better World

JAMES W. MINTON, SR. (JIM)

WESTBOW
PRESS®
A DIVISION OF THOMAS NELSON
& ZONDERVAN

This book is a work of non-fiction. Unless otherwise noted, the author and the publisher make no explicit guarantees as to the accuracy of the information contained in this book and in some cases, names of people and places have been altered to protect their privacy.

WestBow Press books may be ordered through booksellers or by contacting:

WestBow Press
A Division of Thomas Nelson & Zondervan
1663 Liberty Drive
Bloomington, IN 47403
www.westbowpress.com
1 (866) 928-1240

Because of the dynamic nature of the Internet, any web addresses or links contained in this book may have changed since publication and may no longer be valid. The views expressed in this work are solely those of the author and do not necessarily reflect the views of the publisher, and the publisher hereby disclaims any responsibility for them.

Interior Image Credit: Quincie McCalla

ISBN: 978-1-9736-5082-9 (sc)
ISBN: 978-1-9736-5083-6 (e)

Library of Congress Control Number: 2019900418

Print information available on the last page.

WestBow Press rev. date: 1/28/2019

**LIFE is** preparation **4 e†ernity** but **YOU** have a **PURPOSE** on earth

Phillipians 1:21 | Rick Warren
Ephesians 2:8-10 | Amazing Grace

---

*Life isn't fair*

**BE** a good **winner** a good **loser**

*Go from failure to failure without a loss of enthusiasm.*

Job 11 | Trevor Bayne

---

GOOD BETTER **BEST**

Don't lie, cheat, or steal

DEVELOP GOOD *Habits*

when complain, or make excuses

**Be a good listener**

---

**WORD** entertainment
↓
**WORLD** entertainment

Romans 1:16
Proverbs 14:12

Garbage **IN**  Garbage **OUT**

---

*Have a* **WORD**view

~~FLESH~~ **SPIRIT**

Romans 8:5-8

---

**DON'T BE A VICTIM**

*Things turn out best for those that make the best of the way things turn out.*

John 9:3 | Inky Johnson
The Collins Family | Nick Vujicic

---

*Serve* rather than *Deserve*

Phillipians 2:5-8 | Ephesians 6:7

---

**PREPARE** for *Opportunities*

Colossians 3:23
Galatians 1:10
Proverbs 16:9

---

**RESPECT** **AUTHORITY**

2 Timothy 2:5
Proverbs 1:7, 3:7

 Umpires & Sports Officials

---

DON'T LOSE **HEAVEN** WHEN YOU'RE GOING THROUGH **HELL**

John 16:33 | Psalm 105:19

**Leo Johnson**

---

*Forgive*

Matthew West | Monty Williams

1 John 1:9
Ephesians 4:32
Colossians 3:13

---

**CHRISTIANS** are not **PERFECT,** ── just ── **FORGIVEN**

*Why am I a Christian? Because it is true.*

Luke 23:43

## Acknowledgments

Thanks go out to Cindy Wene and Matthew R. Stolz for all their hard work in preparing this book for publication.

# Contents

# Introduction

*"Your greatest contribution to the kingdom of God might not be something you do, but someone you raise."--Andy Stanley*

*"I have no greater joy than to hear that my children are walking in the truth."--3 John 1:4 NIV*

*"Love the Lord your God with all your heart and with all your soul and with all your strength. These commandments that I give you today are to be on your hearts. **Impress them on your children.** Talk about them when you sit at home and when you walk along the road, when you lie down and when you get up. Tie them as symbols on your hands and bind them on your foreheads. Write them on the doorframes of your houses and on your gates."--Deuteronomy 6:5-9 NIV*

Of all things I have been in my life, there's nothing I enjoy more than being a dad. Now I am getting a taste of the grandpa thing as well, but that falls in the same category.

My first child, J. J., didn't get the best end of the dad deal. He was my learning experience, or should I say failing experience. I had a really hard time going from being a very competitive athlete to being the father of the athlete. It is hard to believe at this point that back then I was *that* dad--the one who yelled and screamed at the ball games. I will never forget the time after a freshman basketball game when J. J. looked at me and said,

"You know, you're not helping." That began a realization that I needed to do some work on my "daddying." However, I really didn't mellow out much during the rest of J. J.'s high school years. I am sure his coaches had a thing or two to say about me.

Suzanne and I were married when J. J. was 3. Kurtis came along when J. J. was 10, soon followed by Emily. By the time they started school, I had had time to mellow and to learn from my mistakes.

Kids can be successful in all sorts of ways. First and foremost, you know they are turning out well when they are a joy for other people to be around. At the end of this chapter, I will show you a Bible verse that is good to use as a report card, to measure your kids' progress and your own success in parenting.

For purposes of credibility, and to brag a little bit, let me tell you about a few of Kurtis' and Emily's accomplishments.

One moment that really took things to the next level was when Kurtis got the results of his ACT college entrance exam. There are lots of standards to use in judging the success of our kids. In this book, we will discuss famous basketball coach John Wooden's definition of success, which says you need to be the best that you can be. God made us all different in our sizes and shapes, and we all have different abilities. As we go through this book, I will spend a lot of time talking about using God's standards as to what success is. But if we used earthly standards, what a proud moment when Kurtis revealed that he got a thirty-two on the ACT. That put him in the top 2 percent of kids taking the college entrance exam.

My wife Suzanne and I both have college degrees, but we were nowhere close to being in the top 2 percent. A lot more of the credit probably belongs to the Lutheran school and St. Teresa High School. Of course, the most credit goes to Kurtis for doing the hard work, but if I am going to get you to pay attention for the next 200 pages, I thought I should share some of our parenting success.

Donald Trump's presidential slogan in 2016 is "Make American Great Again." I believe what makes America great is our commitment to family and to making this country a better place for our kids than we had it. There is a meme currently floating around the internet (possibly based on a Carlos Slim quote) that says, "Instead of leaving a better world for our kids, how about leaving better kids for our world?" **Can you imagine how great the world would be if everyone could get their kids to turn out better than they were?**

Using these earthly standards, the jury is still out on my kids. At this point, Kurtis still needs to graduate from college and get a job. He isn't perfect; he has and will make mistakes along the way, but at least in one way of keeping score, my wife and I felt pretty successful when we heard that ACT test score. We were equally proud, when our daughter Emily followed that up with a thirty on *her* ACT and like Kurtis was also an Illinois State Scholar.

More than just worldly success, however, was when they were able to share their faiths. One of our most blessed moments with Emily went back to her eighth grade graduation when she gave the valedictorian speech. Kurtis had set the bar the year before, as he also was at the top of his class. The last two paragraphs of his speech went like this:

> We have come a long way since we began at this school, but we must realize that though things are changing, we still must continue to become better students, better Christians, and better people. My dad has taught me, "Good, better, best, never let it rest, till your good becomes better, and your better becomes best." We must never be satisfied with where we are, because where we are is nothing compared to where we will be when we are with Jesus in Heaven. I often

see LSA [Lutheran School Association] football shirts that say "Do work" or baseball shirts with Colossians 3:23 [NIV, paraphrased], "Work at everything with all your heart as for working for the Lord not for men." The LSA has given all of us a great education and, most importantly, an education that keeps Christ in the equation. Now I think it's time that we use what we've learned to do God's work.

Our world doesn't need a superhero to change the world, just average people doing what God has put them here to do. I think the movie *Evan Almighty* is right when it says, "We change the world by completing one **A**ct of **R**andom **K**indness at a time," and I think everything can start with us. It doesn't take money or fame. It takes us, the people that God created Himself, doing their part. The LSA has helped by giving us the tools, now it's time for us to do God's work.

As stated at the beginning, there is no greater joy than to know your kids are walking in the truth and have grasped what you have been trying to teach them.

But now it was Emily's turn, and she followed up with this speech:

I have also found a great friend in Jesus here at the LSA. I am so blessed to have a school where I can learn about God and strengthen my faith. As kindergartners, we sang songs like "Jesus Loves Me." One of my dad's favorite authors is Rick Warren. He wrote in his book, *The Purpose Driven Life*, that life basically comes down to two things, our relationship with others and our relationship with Christ. He wrote that knowing and loving God is our greatest privilege, and being known and loved is God's greatest pleasure. God planned the universe and orchestrated history so that we would all be here at the LSA together, so that we could become friends with each other, but also friends with Him. Our purpose is to share that love, so that others will also become God's friends. Proverbs 16:3 [NLT, paraphrased] says, "Commit to the Lord whatever you do and your plans will succeed."

Even if some of us continue life's journey at another school, it is important that God remains first in our every thought, word and action. To have a good friend is one of the highlights of life. To be a good friend is one of the noblest and most difficult undertakings. Often when my parents dropped me off for school, they would ask to make sure I had everything I needed, and many times their last words would be, "Be a good friend."

So many times my spirits have been lifted when I have heard from some of you. I hope somewhere along the way I have been a good friend to you as well. A good friend is someone who will listen, someone whom you can share your deepest thoughts with, someone who brings out the best in you. They make you laugh a little louder and smile a little brighter. They know how crazy you can be and still choose to be seen with you in public. I cannot imagine life without this school or without any one of my classmates. We are blessed to live in an age when no matter where we are, it is easy to stay in touch through things like Facebook and texting. We need to make sure we keep Jesus on our friends list as well. Make sure we go to him when we are faced with life's challenges. He wants to be included in every activity, every conversation, every problem and every celebration. An old hymn states, "What a friend we have in Jesus, all our sins and griefs to bear, what a privilege to carry everything to God in prayer." I end with the words to one of my favorite songs: "We live. We love. We forgive and never give up, 'cause the days we are given are gifts from above. Today we remember to live and to love" [Superchick, "We Live"].

These speeches felt like points where Kurtis and Emily were no longer tagging along with our faith. They were now developing their own faith.

The numbers are telling us that a significant percentage of kids don't do that. They grow up in the church but they never really grasp on to what the church is all about. Then when they get out in the public, they are easily led astray. We often ask why or how kids lose their faith. My guess is they never really had it to begin with. At some point, kids have to go from being part of their family's faith, to having their own.

**It is not what you do for your children, but what you have taught them to do for themselves, that will make them successful human beings.--Ann Landers.**

One of the themes of this book will be: If you give a person a fish, you have fed them for a day, but if you can teach them to fish, they are fed for a lifetime.

There are always people who are better or worse at something. I'm writing this book to try to help people who would be happy with the level of success that I've had in raising my kids.

In 2017, I came up with a new measurement of child-rearing success, when I reached out to Tom Zobrist, father of Chicago Cubs player and World Series MVP Ben Zobrist. My son Kurtis now plays baseball at Olivet Nazarene University, which is where Ben played for three years. The father of one of Kurtis' roommates also happens to be a lifelong friend of Tom's. Through these connections, I invited Tom to come to Decatur and speak at my church.

It's very interesting to interact with Tom, because he is so humble and what I would call a totally normal guy. He is the pastor of a church in the small town of Eureka, Illinois, but he was able to raise a kid who became a World Series MVP. By my standards, it doesn't get much better, but when Tom began his talk at Saint Paul's Lutheran Church that day, he quickly put my thinking in place. He said that people come up to him all the time and ask, "How is your boy doing?" To which he replies, "Which one? I have three of them." Tom considers *all* of his children to be MVPs; Ben just does it on the stage that is most visible.

He went on to tell an amazing story of how he and his wife Cyndi were actually raising Ben to be a preacher. When Tom was going through Bible college, his young children would help him do his homework. By the age of three, Ben had a good grasp of who Jesus was. Ben always had a good way with people and a good relationship with his Lord and Savior, Jesus Christ.

In high school, Ben successfully played three sports, with his greatest achievements actually being in basketball. As graduation approached, his parents were very thankful that Ben seemed ready to go to Bible college and fulfill his parents' dream of him being a preacher.

However, it turned out that their plans and God's plans were a bit different. Ben used fifty dollars of his own birthday money to go to a baseball tryout camp. Out of that camp, he was offered the chance to play baseball at Olivet Nazarene University. His parents had doubts if this was the right thing for Ben, or if he would be better off at Bible college. Ben went on to play for

Olivet for 3 years and then finished up his college career at Dallas Baptist. He was then drafted in the sixth round by the Houston Astros, and the rest is history, 108 years in the making.

Tom finished his talk with a reference to Bible verses about ministering before kings. Ben has been given a huge platform to share the gospel, bigger than his parents could have ever dreamed. In late 2016, Ben went with the Cubs to visit President Obama at the White House. Not long after that, he was asked to give the opening prayer at the National Prayer Breakfast. He sat at the head table, a few places down from President Trump.

I was floored when Tom talked about attending all seven games of the World Series. He went into extra detail about the very last game, played in Cleveland. In the extra innings, Cubs center fielder Albert Almora tagged up and went to second base. Tom quickly realized that meant the Indians would walk slugger Anthony Rizzo and that Ben would be up, putting him in a situation that many kids dream of: the at bat that could win the World Series or lose it. After getting down by two strikes, Ben was able to lash a ball down the third base line, scoring the go-ahead run. What an incredible moment for his proud parents!

In October of 2017, Tom released a book, *The Zobrist Family: Look What God Can Do*, that includes these stories.

Yet as Tom mentioned, he looks on all of his kids as MVPs. It's great if your kids can have worldly success in this life, but how do you define true success? One simple yet very powerful way is to apply 1 Corinthians 13:4-8 NIV:

> Love is patient, love is kind. It does not envy, it does not boast, it is not proud. It does not dishonor others, it is not self-seeking, it is not easily angered, it keeps no record of wrongs. Love does not delight in evil but rejoices with the truth. It always protects, always trusts, always hopes, always perseveres. Love never fails.

Now take your child's name, and insert it into each point of this verse. Does this verse now describe your kid?

| | |
|---|---|
| _____ | is patient |
| _____ | is kind |
| _____ | does not envy |
| _____ | does not boast |
| _____ | is not proud |
| _____ | does not dishonor others |
| _____ | is not self seeking |
| _____ | is not easily angered |
| _____ | does not delight in evil, but rejoices in the truth |
| _____ | always protects |
| _____ | always trusts |
| _____ | always hopes |
| _____ | always perseveres |
| _____ | never fails |

When I was ten years old, I had life all figured out. My brother's friends called me "the Professor" because I would sit at his basketball games and broadcast them into a recorder, while keeping stats during the course of the game. At that young age, I could talk sports with the best of them. My life plan was to play professional baseball for ten years and then get into broadcasting. At MacArthur High School, I batted .532 in my senior year, which in 2017 was still standing as the best average in the forty year history of the school. I landed a scholarship to Georgia Southern, which at the time was one of the top twenty-five baseball schools in the country. I have a letter stating that they wanted me to take the place of Marty Pevey, who was getting drafted that year. Marty went on to play in the major leagues and is currently the manager of the Iowa Cubs. At the last minute, I decided not to move sixteen hours away from home and contacted Tom Dedin at Illinois to let him know I was ready to accept their scholarship offer. However, they had already committed to another player, so

Tom put me in touch with the coaches at St. Xavier in Chicago. I ended up there, playing baseball and studying communications.

After my freshman year, I was still young enough to play Legion ball. I was part of the best Legion team to play in Decatur, as we finished second in the Illinois state tournament and the Central Plains Regional. I was named MVP of the state tourney and was able to meet many valuable people that would be a part of my life, including Kevin Koslofski.

After so many successes and a promising future in sports, I'm sure my parents were pretty disappointed when I announced in my junior year of college that I was going to be a dad. It's interesting how life works. **What at the time seemed like a mistake is now what I am writing about as my greatest pleasure.** There have been times that life has been awfully hard. JJ's mom and I ended up divorced, and it is never easy to raise a kid in two houses and two families. However, now I can't imagine life without James Walter "J. J." Minton Jr., even more so since he has made me a grandfather with his own sons, Noah and Elijah. I am so proud of the dad J. J. has become and of the fact that he is building his home to change the world.

So with all this in mind, let me share this little blueprint with you:

**Build the home! Change the world!**

I believe that this world would be a better place if we got back to traditional family values. I would like to see kids growing up in homes where they are receiving love from both a mom and a dad who have established a stable life together, homes where kids are introduced to reading and writing at an early age, homes where, from proper discipline and parents' examples, kids learn the basics of being a good citizen: Don't cheat, lie or steal, and don't whine, complain or make excuses for your actions.

In this better world, kids wake up each day thankful that they get to live in a country with the opportunities and blessings of the USA. By the time they get to high school, they have developed good habits in their eating, studying and work ethics. They have so much invested in their studies and their chosen sports or extracurricular activities that it is easy to say no to drugs, alcohol, sex and other immoral behavior that could put them behind the eight-ball as they go forward.

After finishing their schooling and establishing a way to make a living, these well-grounded young people save up some money before deciding to marry their long-time sweethearts. After a few honeymoon years, it will be their turn to be the parents and pass on the traditional family values that they were taught.

Obviously, we are all going to make mistakes and hit some bumps as we travel down this road. But it is important that we establish what are the right and wrong paths, so we know if we are headed in a good direction. It is my hope that with the thirteen principles I discuss in this book, I will give you some tools you can use to put this goal into motion.

If we build the home, we can change the world!

# Have a WORDview.

*"Those who live according to the flesh have their minds set on what the flesh desires; but those who live in accordance with the Spirit have their minds set on what the Spirit desires. The mind governed by the flesh is death, but the mind governed by the Spirit is life and peace. The mind governed by the flesh is hostile to God; it does not submit to God's law, nor can it do so. Those who are in the realm of the flesh cannot please God."--Romans 8:5-8 NIV*

*"If we never stop and examine our worldview, we'll still have one, but it may not be the right one."--John Stonestreet, President, Colson Center for Christian Worldview*

### Do we need God to be good people?

If you would not title yourself as a Christian conservative, you may want to read this chapter last. While the entire book is based upon Biblical principles, this chapter also includes a political angle. It seems that many people today look through their political glasses as the most important part of how they see the world. I know I am guilty of that on many occasions.

According to the American Humanist website, humanism is a progressive philosophy of life that, without theism and other supernatural beliefs, affirms our ability and responsibility to lead ethical lives of personal fulfillment that aspire to the greater good of humanity.

In Matthew 22 and Mark 12, Jesus gives us the two great commands to love God and to love our neighbor. It seems to me that today we are getting better at the second one, but it is at the expense of the first one.

## What is a worldview?

The Merriam-Webster dictionary defines it this way: "a comprehensive conception or apprehension of the world especially from a specific standpoint." I like to describe a worldview as the type of glasses through which your kids view life.

Some people have a worldview of, "He who dies with the most toys wins." An atheist believes that, "This life is all there is, so you better make the most of it."

There are all kinds of humanist approaches, about as many as there are religions, but I think you can sum up the worldview of a humanist as: We can be good without God.

According to the website cited above, humanism teaches us that it is immoral to wait for God to act for us. We must act to stop the wars and the crimes and the brutality of this and future ages. We have powers of a remarkable kind. We have a high degree of freedom in choosing what we will do. Humanism tells us that whatever our philosophy of the universe may be, ultimately the responsibility for the kind of world in which we live rests with us.

If you look at our public schools, they are teaching some form of humanism. God and religion are not allowed, but the schools are still hoping to make good people. Is that working? I could throw you out some figures, but I am sure you already have your opinion.

Humanism gets scary when you look at the technology we have today. A CBS news article from August 2017 is titled "What kind of society do you want to live in? Inside the country where Down syndrome is disappearing." It sounds pretty positive until you read how they are accomplishing this. The country of Iceland is offering prenatal screening to pregnant women. Eighty to 85 percent will get this done. Close to 100 percent choose to abort the baby if the test comes back positive for Down syndrome. Is it good when we play God? Is it good when we decide which lives have value and which lives don't?

Liberalism is a worldview that breaks down to a couple of goals. They have a belief that if we can just get rid of religions and countries, everyone will be able to get along. They also want to do away with greedy capitalism. If everybody could live at comparable levels, everyone would be equally happy (or equally miserable).

Take a look sometime at the words to John Lennon's song "Imagine".

Have I made you mad yet? If you want to irritate a large number of people these days, start talking politics. It just amazes me how half the country sees things one way and the other half has a totally opposite opinion. Some people see government as the answer. Other people see government as the problem.

I am a Christian conservative. I am not a fan of liberalism or humanism because one of their goals is to get Jesus out of the public square. I believe the answer is, "Build the home! Change the world!" I believe the key, "Better dads, better kids," will get us a better world. We need to get back to traditional family values with the Bible in the center.

Psalm 119 is the longest chapter in the longest book of the Bible. To summarize, it says I will live my life according to Your Word.

**With all of the opposing opinions out there, it is important that your child has a WORDview (i.e. Biblical viewpoint) as opposed to a worldview. Remove one little letter, and it makes all the difference.**

For the most part, there seem to be two approaches to follow today. One is the science-evolution approach that is taught in our schools, and the other is the significant designer approach that is presented by religions.

One of the leaders on the so-called science side is Lawrence Krauss, a theoretical physicist from Arizona State University. He says in a Big Think video, "The picture that science presents to us is . . . uncomfortable because what we've learned is that we are more insignificant than we ever could have imagined. You could get rid of us and all the galaxies and everything we see in the universe, and it would be largely the same. So we are insignificant on a scale that Copernicus never would have imagined, and, in addition, it turns out the future is miserable.... You might think that should depress you, but I would argue that in fact it should embolden you and provide you a different kind of consolation. Because if the universe doesn't care about us and if we're an accident in a remote corner . . . in some sense it makes us more precious. The meaning in our lives is . . . provided by us. We provide our own meaning, and we are here by...accidents of evolution. . . . And we should enjoy our brief moment in the sun. We should make the most of [it] . . . because this is all we have."

I wouldn't expect this approach to play very well when you are trying to figure out the death of a child. How do you get through something like that without the hope of Jesus?

I believe science is trying to figure out what God already knows. I don't see the debate as you have to choose one or the other. Science should be the never-ending effort to make this world a better place by figuring out what God already knows.

If you are trying to figure out how something works on your car, you go to the owner's manual. If you want to figure out how to get from point A to point B, you look at a roadmap. I don't see how you can figure out life without going to the ultimate owner's manual, the Bible.

I would hope that you would give me the opportunity to

explain where I am coming from by reading the rest of this book. As I mentioned in the intro, it has worked out pretty well for me. In Principle #13, I lay out my Christian testimony. When I look at all the evidence, I have come to the conclusion that the God of the Bible is true and that He has set up a certain way for things to work. He was the Creator of your child, so if you are going to understand your child, you must go to the owner's manual. I find it very hard to support the public schools when they have removed the Bible from their curriculum; how can you teach knowledge without it? Look at 1 John 4:4-6 NIV:

> You, dear children, are from God and have overcome them, because the one who is in you is greater than the one who is in the world. They are from the world and therefore speak from the viewpoint of the world, and the world listens to them. We are from God, and whoever knows God listens to us; but whoever is not from God does not listen to us. This is how we recognize the Spirit of truth and the spirit of falsehood.

*Time* magazine rated Jesus as the most significant person in history. Even a magazine that I would consider to be liberal states the importance of Jesus, yet our schools don't teach about Him. I think it is hard for kids to understand life when they are being taught with a wrong owner's manual. Imagine if every time you asked Google Maps a question, you got the wrong answer, and you were sent in a totally inaccurate direction. With the WORDview that is provided by the Bible, our kids have access to a completely reliable source of information for life's questions.

The Bible contains sixty-six books that were written by forty different authors. Dr. Voddie Baucham, Jr., is a pastor and author with an emphasis on apologetics. In an article by Butch Blume, Dr. Baucham describes the Bible this way: "[I]t is a reliable collection of historical documents written by eyewitnesses during the lifetime of other eye witnesses. They report supernatural events that took place in fulfillment of specific prophecies and claimed that their writings are divine rather than human in origin." Many of these authors were willing to die for what they wrote.

In Principle #13, I mention the Dead Sea Scrolls, which provided us with one of the oldest versions of the book of Isaiah. This book does an amazing job of telling us what was going to happen in the New Testament. As you study the verses of Isaiah, you see how practical this book is for life today.

So the Bible is not only a reliable document of the history of Jesus, it is also a very practical guide for day-to-day life. As you go through these principles, you will see a variety of Bible verses used to make key points.

## Are we a Christian nation?

According to the History Channel website (A&E Television Networks, LLC), "In God We Trust" became the US Motto in 1956. According to the Florida Department of State's website, "In God We Trust" has been Florida's motto since 1868. (The state's motto started out as "In God is our Trust.") In 2006, Florida reconfirmed "In God We Trust" as their motto.

The first commandment says we shall have no other gods. We are shocked and horrified by the tragedy of Las Vegas in 2017, as well we should be, but that same event occurs every weekend in our big cities. Kids are killing each other at staggering rates. According to Reuters.com, Chicago had over 500 deaths in 2017. Our response has been to protest the police.

Luther's catechism defines the first commandment as we should fear, love and trust in God above all things. God doesn't tell us that to be some evil dictator. He tells us that as the designer of this universe and the designer of the people who live in it. When we worship things other than God, we end up with a bad result. Just like good parents set out a series of guidelines as to how their kids should behave, God has set out a set of guidelines for us.

In Exodus 20, God lays out a set of rules for the Israelites. They had been in slavery and wandered in the wilderness. Now it was time for them to rule themselves.

Today our country has decided to get in line with the rest of the world with a motto that goes something like this. Tolerance is the new golden rule. As Ron Rhodes expresses it, "Be tolerant of others (their beliefs, actions, and lifestyle) as you would have them be tolerant of you (your beliefs, actions, and lifestyle)-- *for all beliefs, actions and lifestyles are equally valid* [italics in original]."

Of course, that means they are tolerant of everything that isn't Christian. According to Jay Reeves of the *Chicago Tribune*, Christian organizations, like D. James Kennedy Ministries, are being labeled as a hate group because they support the Biblical definition of marriage.

The Ten Commandments in Exodus 20 are a great place to help your child start their "WORDview."

Legendary coach John Wooden, well known for his inspirational quotes, was taught by his father, Josh Wooden, "two sets of threes" that provide a good framework for daily life (from *Wooden*):

|  |  |
|---|---|
| Never lie. | Don't whine. |
| Never cheat. | Don't complain. |
| Never steal. | Don't make excuses. |

You don't have to teach kids how to sin. Their nature is to whine, complain and make excuses. It is normal for them to want to bend the rules or take the easiest way in an effort to get ahead. It's fun to point the fingers at our kids, but if we are honest, it is always true of who we are.

I think these "two sets of threes" are an important tool to have in your parental arsenal. My wife and I kept them posted on the refrigerator. As we went about daily life, I listened to the kids talking about their various situations. I would listen intently, but at some point, I would slip in, "Are you done whining?" With Kurtis, I would sometimes tease him by saying, "You finally did it! You came up with the good excuse."

It's important that we give our kids an "I can" attitude. It is human nature to come up with reasons why we can't, usually in the form of good excuses, so when your family is together in the kitchen, quickly review the "two sets of threes." Encourage everyone to be a family that doesn't whine, complain or make excuses. In Principle #11, I talk about how if I were God, I would do things differently. When we whine and complain, we are telling God that He isn't doing it right, that if we were in control of the universe, we could set up a better scenario for our lives.

*Do not conform to the pattern of this world, but be transformed by the renewing of your mind.*
*--Romans 12:2 NIV*

Jay Carty does a great job with this topic in the devotional book that he wrote with Coach Wooden, *Coach Wooden One-on-One*:

> Joseph was sold into slavery by his brothers and thrown into jail unjustly. He didn't whine or complain. God rewarded him. Jacob tricked his brother, Esau, but a trickier trickster named Laban tricked the trickster. Jacob didn't whine or complain. God rewarded him. It was the same way with Job. He did just fine with all his troubles until he started whining and complaining. God got on his case. It appears that God doesn't like

grousing, but what about making excuses? What was the first thing Eve did after sinning? She blamed the snake. What's the first thing Adam did? He blamed Eve. When that didn't work, he blamed God. "It was the woman *You* gave me." So God gave them both the boot. He doesn't like excuses for sin [italics in original].

The liberal worldview that our kids are being taught today often revolves around rights. Everybody has a right to live life the way they want. Everyone has a right to quality healthcare. If you have an "unwanted" pregnancy, it is your right to end it. You attend protests to demand your rights.

What this worldview gives you the right to do is to complain about your circumstances. When you complain, you end up with a glass that is half empty. Next thing you know, you make things worse than they really are, and instead of taking advantages of opportunities, you are spending your time and effort saying, "Poor me."

In the *Coach Wooden One-on-One* devotional, Coach Wooden states:

> **I'm convinced we do too much for others, and I think it has hurt our nation.** I know it has hurt our society and our families. When you do too much, neither countries nor people appreciate it. If people are hungry, give them fish. But after they have eaten, teach them how to fish. Don't keep giving them fish. That makes them dependent on you for their food. It's never good to take away anyone's independence.... The only dependence I wanted my loved ones to have was dependence on God, and I wanted them to have Jesus in their hearts [emphasis added].

As Christians with a WORDview, we really should learn and focus on all Ten Commandments. But Wooden's "two sets of threes" give us a quick synopsis.

Do you remember when the Joneses were just people that lived a couple of doors down? Now, it is all about being able to keep up with them. For one of the first times in history, we have decisions to make about how we live our lives. When we gathered and hunted, that took up most of our time. When we grew up on the farm, we often had to figure out how to make the best of our circumstances. We were limited in our interaction with others, but we learned a great deal about hard work. Today we don't have to spend a lot of times on the basics of life. We actually have the chance to decide how we are going to consume things.

It would be great if this book would present the gospel to some people who don't currently have Christ in their life, who came here looking for parenting advice and walked away with a Savior, but who I really want to address in this book is the 70 to 80% of people in this country who call themselves Christian.

In a recent study, the Barna Group revealed a stunning statistic that continues to reverberate throughout the evangelical world. Only 9% of professing Christians have a biblical worldview. The number is much worse for those eighteen to twenty-three years of age.

> For the purposes of the survey, a "biblical worldview" was defined as believing that absolute moral truth exists; the Bible is totally accurate in all of the principles it teaches; Satan is considered to be a real being or force, not merely symbolic; a person cannot earn their way into Heaven by trying to be good or do good works; Jesus Christ lived a sinless life on Earth; and God is the all-knowing, all-powerful creator of the world who still rules the universe today. In

the research, anyone who held all of those beliefs
was said to have a biblical worldview.

Because of this, many of today's believers live very similarly to non-believers. A personal sense of significance is rarely experienced. We spend our money and time on things that fail to satisfy, and we begin to wonder what life's ultimate purpose really is. We are, in short, losing our bearings as a people and a nation. When we read Romans 8:5, we can't seem to apply it to our own lives.

Most everything you do with your kids will be caught not taught. If you don't know your Bible, odds are your kids won't learn the Bible. If you have trouble controlling your bad habits, your kids will probably have trouble controlling theirs as well.

In Principle #8, I will talk about having a "serve rather than deserve" attitude. Most people define success by how many people serve them. A much better way to approach life is by counting how many people you serve.

### Does your life line up with God's vision?

From day one, kids are messy. It's our job to clean them up. Your worldview, how you see things, drives your behavior. Most physicians recognize that they don't cure the human body. They provide favorable circumstances through treatments and recommendations, so that God's great creation, the human body, can cure itself. Our mission as parents involves removing roadblocks in our family so that God can be God. We need to follow his roadmap, the Bible, in order to get our kids where we would like for them to go.

**My goal is to help you establish a game plan so that your family has a Christian worldview, a WORDview.** A WORDview is a Biblically-based way of looking at things. The old adage that Wooden made reference to earlier is that if you give a man a fish, you feed him for a day, but if you can teach that man to fish, you have fed him for a lifetime. It is my hope and prayer that this book will help you set your kids' inner compasses to the right direction, that it will give them decision-making tools and get them in a frame of mind where they don't need you to fix their every little move. They will have the means to make their own good decisions and grow into good, law-abiding, tax-paying citizens, who then go on to provide you with some wonderful grandchildren.

Most parents target symptoms and behaviors. They become fatigued putting out fires, but fail to take the matches away.

If you can establish the "two sets of threes" for your kids and ingrain the thirteen principles of this book, your kids will have a much better chance of being successful in what really matters in life.

God is more interested in your character than in your comfort. Your reputation is how others perceive you, but your character is how you really are. There are only two beings who really know your character--you and God. To paraphrase a quote attributed to Abraham Lincoln, you can fool most of the people some of the time. However, you can't fool yourself, and you certainly can't fool God.

Most of us want comfort at all costs. The world is telling our kids they deserve these comforts, and if someone short-changes you, then you have the right to kick up a fuss and demand more.

When we pray, first and foremost we should pray that God's will be done. In the Lord's Prayer, we pray that God's will would be done on Earth as it is in Heaven. Most of us pray for personal blessings or to fix broken situations, but prayer should mostly be about getting your attitude lined up with God's attitude.

The entire Bible is about people falling over and over again into their sinful natures. They always want to find a way to Heaven on Earth. In the eleventh principle, we will take a look at one of my sayings that I seem to use constantly: "There is Heaven. There is hell. There is Earth, with a little bit of both."

We constantly tell God that we have figured out a better way. Thankfully, God always takes us back when we discover that our ways don't work.

## The world at its worst needs the family at its best.

Philippians 2:3-4 NIV says, "Do nothing out of selfish ambition or vain conceit. Rather, in humility value others above yourselves, not looking to your own interests but each of you to the interests of others."

> "Humility is not thinking less of yourself; it is thinking of yourself less."--Rick Warren

John Wooden has written a great deal about success. He defines success in terms of being the best that you can be. In his book, *Wooden*, he gives the following definition: "Success is peace of mind that is a direct result of self-satisfaction in knowing you did your best to become the best you are capable of becoming." He learned this from his father, who often stated that you should never try to be better than someone else. However, he didn't stop there; he went on to say that you should never stop trying to be the best that you can be.

The story of Joshua Wooden, John's father, is an interesting one. The man failed at many things. He lost his farm during the Great Depression, and it was a struggle to feed his family. He fed them with more important things, however, with wisdom and good books, especially the Bible.

This book started with Andy Stanley's thought that your greatest accomplishment in life may not be something you do but someone you raise. Joshua Wooden was a failure by some standards, but he raised one of the wisest men to ever live. John Wooden had incredible success as a basketball coach, but more importantly, he had incredible success as a teacher of life.

Jesus certainly had a WORDview when he went to the cross. Talk about putting character before comfort! His life demonstrated that he was always willing to sacrifice for others. **Jesus makes it clear that sacrifice is essential for being his follower.**

This isn't easy to teach today. We even have churches that preach the prosperity gospel. There were a lot of lessons that occurred when kids grew up on the farm, when it was natural for a family to work together. Today's culture is giving kids a different lesson, one that tells them they should expect a certain level of living. We are blessed to have a lot of instant gratification in today's society, but when we get used to that, it adds to our "deserve" attitude. Burger King knew what they were doing when they developed the slogan, "Have it your way." These attitudes have led our kids down a difficult path.

It also was easier back when TV shows helped with parenting, as opposed to hurting. One of the all-time greats was *The Andy Griffith Show*, where an entertaining story would end with Andy teaching a life lesson to his son, Opie. One of the best episodes was "Opie and the Spoiled Kid."

In this episode, Opie is impressed by a new bike a kid is riding. This kid then convinces Opie that his dad is doing a number on him by only giving him a quarter for his allowance and making him clean the garage in order to earn that quarter. The kid teaches Opie the latest tricks for getting his way, including holding his breath and throwing tantrums.

When the kid gets in trouble for riding his bike on the sidewalk, his dad quickly takes his side. But when the father tells Sheriff Andy that he is being unfair, Andy responds, "If we don't teach kids to live in society today, what is going to happen when they grow up?"

After the kid pitches a fit and is willing to let his dad go to jail so he can get his bike back, the father finally comes to his senses. He gives the kid some discipline, and Opie realizes how out of line he has been. I think this episode is a good summary of today's liberal worldview.

Christian author and speaker Dr. Kevin Leman has written a series of books on raising kids. Many of his teachings have become part of my thought process. One of the best things that happened to me as a parent was attending a program at my church that was based on Dr. Leman's book *Making Children Mind without Losing Yours*.

Dr. Leman opened his class with Ephesians 6:1-4 NKJV, "Children, obey your parents in the Lord, for this is right. 'Honor your father and mother,' which is the first commandment with promise: 'that it may be well with you and you may live long on the earth.' And you, fathers, do not provoke your children to wrath, but bring them up in the training and admonition of the Lord." He finishes with a great statement that he credits to evangelical author Josh McDowell: **"Rules without relationships lead to rebellion."**

In the first portion of Leman's class, the focus was on "reality discipline." That is the action-oriented way to make your children accountable for their actions. The ultimate goal of reality discipline is to enable the child to deal in practical ways with the reality of the authority of God, established in and through Jesus Christ.

Proverbs has a bunch of good verses on discipline, starting with Proverbs 22:6 KJV, "Train up a child in the way he should go, and when he is old he will not depart from it." If you want to "build the home and change the world," read a chapter in Proverbs every day. It just so happens that there are thirty-one chapters in this book, so take a couple of the months with thirty-one days and focus on this as Bible study.

**Who is the authority in your house? Your life should not revolve around the child.** He or she should not be the one in authority.

Leman also answered the question, "Why do kids misbehave?"

Usually, he said, it is one of three reasons: attention, power or revenge. My viewpoint is that if you don't get misbehavior under control, then it becomes a habit. Then, when it becomes a child's habitual response, it's really hard to fight, and you end up with the spoiled or rebellious brat.

Also, if we right all the wrongs in our kids' lives, they are going to have a tough time coping when they are adults. (Leman was great with funny quips; he illustrated this bad parenting method with, "Would you kids turn the TV down in there? I'm trying to do your homework!") Kids have to learn that there are consequences to their actions.

Relationship is the key to teaching your kids. I remember a situation when Emily was about ten years old; she threw a temper tantrum and locked herself in her bedroom. There needed to be consequences for those actions, but I also thought it was a good time to show her that I cared. Kids don't care how much you know, until you show how much you care, so I slipped a note under the door. I can't remember what the question was that I asked her, but she wrote on the note and slid it back under the door to me. After many minutes and a few more notes, her tantrum was over. If I had just left the situation alone, I might have empowered her to face future frustrations with the same bad actions. Instead, we took the time to discuss the situation, and she learned how to handle things differently.

Children need guidance. They want you around, even if they say they don't. It's important to be able to read your kids and take advantage of times when they are in the mood to listen. If a kid feels wronged, you might not be able to get through to them at that moment. Later, however, when it's time for a little ice cream and they are in a better frame of mind, it is the perfect time to go back and revisit their episode.

I like to tease. That has helped me build a relationship with my kids, but I've found it doesn't work very well with sensitive kids or those with ADHD or high energy levels. You have to figure out what works, in order to approach your kids appropriately to get the desired outcome.

In Dr. Leman's class, two extreme parenting styles were presented. The authoritarian parent makes all the decisions for the child. These parents use reward and punishment to control the child's behavior and see themselves as better than the child. They run the home with an iron hand and grant little freedom to the child. On the other side is the permissive parent, who is a slave to the child. These parents place their priority on the child, not on their spouse. They rob the child of self-respect and self-esteem by doing things that the child can do for him or herself. **They provide the child with the Disneyland experience**, making things as easy as possible. This style invites rebellion, due to inconsistent parenting.

In between these two extremes is the authoritative, or responsible, parenting model. This parent gives the child choices and formulates guidelines with him or her. The parent provides the child with decision-making opportunities, develops consistent, loving discipline and holds the child accountable. An authoritative parent lets reality be the teacher and conveys respect, self-worth and love to the child. This parenting style enhances the child's self-esteem.

Dr. Leman's teachings encouraged me to share my own imperfections with my kids. I wanted my kids to know that I was on their team. I wanted them to win, but part of that was to put them back in place when they got out of line. I also often told them, "Do as I say, not as I do." I wanted them to know that I struggled with my sinful self as well, and we would work together to live up to God's standards.

Abraham Lincoln has been quoted as saying, "The worst thing you can do for those you love is the things they could and should do for themselves." (As historian Edward Steers, Jr., points out, the original quote was by the Reverend William John Henry Boetcker and a bit different.) There were so many times that I wished I had the money to do a great deal more for my kids, but in the end, I may have done a great deal more for my kids because I didn't have the means to spoil them.

Church was always a great place for our kids to learn. They didn't get much out of the sermons when they were little, but what they did learn was to sit still and not interrupt Mommy and Daddy while they were worshiping. This is the sort of modeling that needs to be done in a multitude of areas. I always find it frustrating when, five minutes into the sermon, a kid has to use the bathroom and causes a disruption. A parent should be smart enough to pick up on this behavior and address it before the service starts.

Our goal with our kids should be to teach them to fish, as opposed to constantly having to give them fish. To do that, we need to get our kids to put on their WORDview glasses. When the world starts telling our children that its way is better and they should demand more from others, it is our job as parents to keep them focused on the long term.

# Life is preparation for eternity, but you have a purpose here on Earth.

*"It ought to be the business of every day to prepare for our last day."--Matthew Henry*

Life is preparation for eternity. I love the old hymn that is a favorite in the Lutheran Church: "I'm But a Stanger Here (Heaven is My Home)."

*"That, be assured, is the great Easter truth. Not that we are to live newly after death--that is not the great thing--but that we are to be new here and now by the power of the resurrection."*
*--Phillips Brooks*

*"It has been said that the two most important days of a man's life are the day on which he was born and the day on which he discovers why he was born."--Unknown*

You have probably heard of Stephen Covey's book, *The 7 Habits of Highly Effective People.* The second habit Covey discusses is, "Begin with the end in mind." It is the ability to envision in your mind what you cannot at present see with your eyes. It is based on the principle that all things are created twice: once in your head or on paper and then once in reality. If you were to construct a building, you would follow a blueprint. If you don't make a conscious effort to visualize who you are and what you want in life, i.e. if you don't have a blueprint, then you empower other people and circumstances to shape you and your life by default. It's about connecting again with your own uniqueness, and then defining the personal, moral and ethical guidelines within which you can most happily express and fulfill yourself. Beginning with the end in mind means starting each day, task or project with a clear vision of your desired direction and destination. You then flex your proactive muscles to make things happen.

That sounds really nice on paper, but sometimes things don't work out as you expected or how you drew them up on the paper.

Rick Warren's *The Purpose Driven Life* really helped me to begin with the end in mind, but that end is a life in eternity. The Bible is the owner's manual to life. People basically haven't changed in the last 4,000 years, so though the Bible is the story of Jesus, it also gives us a very good roadmap for how to understand life.

I was really surprised when I started researching near-death experiences after seeing the movie *Heaven is for Real.* These are the experiences of people who have died but been resuscitated. In John Burke's book, *Imagine Heaven,* he documents 120 different stories like this. He was amazed how well the stories lined up with what the Bible says about Heaven. At the very least, many of the stories are still amazing miracles.

One of the stories describes a person who came out of a coma and asked why there were tennis shoes on the roof of the hospital. Sure enough, when people went to look, the shoes were there. In another story, a man had a heart attack during open-heart surgery. When he regained consciousness, the staff apologized for losing his false teeth during the trauma. The man amazed them by saying that the teeth weren't lost, they actually had been placed in the third drawer of the crash cart, and there they were.

These people believe that during their death experiences,

they were sucked out of their earthly bodies and began drifting up towards Heaven. From there, they were able to see what was happening on Earth. Are these stories true?

I do think it is important that we imagine Heaven. It may be that our lives here on Earth are just a few inches of a mile-long rope that is our life and eternity.

Ecclesiastes 3:11 NLT says that God "has planted eternity in the human heart." If you are going to have good kids, I think they have to have a proper WORDview, as described in Principle #1. In order for that to happen, they have to understand that there is more to life than just what we experience here on Earth. Life is preparation for eternity.

*"For instance, we know that when these bodies of ours are taken down like tents and folded away, they will be replaced by resurrection bodies in heaven - God-made, not handmade"*
*--2 Corinthians 5:1 MSG*

In the movie *Toy Story*, Buzz Lightyear uses the phrase, "To infinity and beyond!" How do you go beyond the endless? But you have to love his spirit.

There's a cartoon (based on a short story by Pablo J. Luis Molinero) that pops up on the internet of two babies in the mother's womb. One says to the other, "Do you believe in life outside the womb?" The other baby responds, "No, that is just a myth." Likewise, it is hard for us to imagine that there is life after death. Philippians 1:21 NIV says, "For to me, to live is Christ and to die is gain."

We just have a different approach to life if we are focused on Heaven. We place a higher premium on relationship and character, instead of fame or wealth or achievements or even fun. Philippians 3:7 NLT says, "I once thought these things were valuable, but now I consider them worthless because of what Christ has done."

My life verse is Luke 23:43. This is the verse Pastor Wray Offerman preached at my mom's funeral in 2005. Jesus tells the repentant sinner on the cross, "Today you will be with me in paradise." My mom was a bit infamous for saving seats for her kids at church; we now enjoy talking about the spots that she is saving in Heaven.

> *"In my Father's house are many mansions: if it were not so, I would have told you. I go to prepare a place for you."--John 14:2 KJV*

I have heard it said that if your God is so good and Heaven is his perfect place, why are you here? Why doesn't God immediately take us up to Heaven when we accept his saving grace?

If we are still here on Earth, God has us here for a purpose. It is our job to show Jesus to others. John Wooden is a great example of this. Even after the age of eighty, he was still sharing his wisdom and faith through an amazing number of books. (He and Steve Jamison were putting together a book, *The Wisdom of Wooden: My Century On and Off the Court*, for his one hundredth birthday, but he didn't quite make it there, passing at the age of ninety-nine.)

As *The Purpose Driven Life* helped me understand that life is preparation for eternity, it also helped me realize that I am on Earth for a purpose. Life is not just about me. Life is not an accident. I would highly recommend that you read this book. For many years, I carried around a list of the first line of all forty chapters. You could get a good feel from just reading those lines. Four of my most favorite are:

It's not about you.
You are not an accident.
You were created to become like Christ.
Living on purpose is the only way to really live.

It is so amazing how diverse we are. Even identical twins have different fingerprints. There are over six billion people on this planet, and we can figure out who is who by fingerprints. Technology is also being developed that allows you to be identified by the unique patterns of your retina.

Just like our fingerprints and retinas are different, I think the roles we are supposed to play on Earth are all a bit different as well. Are there jobs here on Earth that only you can do? Are there people who will be in Heaven only if you share the gospel with them?

Ephesians 2:8-10 NIV does a great job in pointing us in the right direction. "For it is by grace you have been saved, through faith--and this is not from yourselves, it is the gift of God--not by works, so that no one can boast. For we are God's handiwork, created in Christ Jesus to do good works, which God prepared in advance for us to do."

Some Christians believe that things are always supposed to go well. However, there are many stories of Christian martyrs, including most of Jesus' disciples.

There is a video on YouTube of gospel singer Wintley Phipps performing on Bill and Gloria Gaither's show. This man's purpose on Earth is to praise God by singing spirituals. I can't do justice to this video in a book, but in this particular performance, he shares that almost all African American spirituals were composed using the black keys of the piano. He plays some examples, "Every Time I Feel the Spirit" and "Swing Low, Sweet Chariot." Phipps says the composers used the black keys because they didn't come to America with "do re mi;" that was someone else's scale. What they used is referred to as the pentatonic scale.

Phipps then proceeds to play "Amazing Grace," calling it a white spiritual played on the black keys. He says if you look up the song, the words are by John Newton, but the composer of the melody is unknown. Newton was the captain of a slave ship and probably heard the tune coming from the belly of the ship.

Phipps says he looks forward to getting to Heaven to meet the unknown authors of this melody.

In the movie *Amazing Grace*, William Wilberforce is a member of the British Parliament, when he experiences a religious enlightenment and aligns himself with the evangelical wing of the Church of England. He thinks about leaving for the ministry, but his friends persuade him that he will be more effective doing the work of God by taking on the abolition of the British slave trade.

Wilberforce's conviction deepens when he meets John Newton, author of the lyrics to "Amazing Grace." Newton tells Wilberforce of all the ghosts that haunt him from his days as a slave ship captain.

The movie then details a number of failures over the next twenty years, before Wilberforce is finally able to accomplish his purpose. He devises a back-door method of slowly convincing his fellow members of Parliament that God created all men equal. They realize that slaves are no different than any other human being in the eyes of God, and the government should treat them the same way.

Also be sure to look up the story of the life purpose of Dietrich Bonhoeffer. He was a German pastor who became a spy against the Nazi army. His writings on Christianity's role in the secular world have become widely influential, and his book *The Cost of Discipleship* has become a modern classic. Hitler convinced the church to look the other way while he killed eleven million Jews. Bonhoeffer tried to point out how unbiblical it was to think a class of people had to be exterminated. Ultimately, Bonhoeffer was put in a concentration camp and executed, shortly before World War II ended.

Bonhoeffer's teachings really resonate today, as once again politics seem to be more important than the church. It would appear that politicians are asking us to change our religious views to fit with their social opinions. In *The Cost of Discipleship*,

Bonhoeffer talked about cheap grace, meaning that people were forgiven for their sins, but they didn't really ever change their lives. Bonhoeffer was pushing people for costly grace, which meant they were willing to stand up for their faith and suffer consequences if necessary.

There is an ESPN video available on Michael Phelps, the Olympic gold medal swimmer. At the age of fifteen, Michael was in his first Olympics. By the time he was done, he had become the most decorated Olympian of all time, winning twenty-eight gold medals. Why would someone like that need God? He has life all figured out, with money and fame to boot. What more could you ask for?

Well, Michael was dogged by his relationship with his father. His parents divorced when he was nine, and his dad wasn't part of his life. Michael longed to have his dad's approval.

When Michael decided to retire from swimming, he suddenly had time on his hands for the first time in his life. I remember watching Golf Channel when Hank Haney tried to teach Michael how to play golf. It was quite interesting to watch this world-class athlete struggle with trying to pick up a new sport.

The Bible says that it is hard for a rich man to get into Heaven. If you have Earth all figured out, you tend not to ask the bigger questions. When people are the center of the universe, they tend to become very focused on themselves. As part of this book, we focus a bit on how it's important to remember that our children are just a part of our lives and not the center. I've mentioned several times that when you were one of six or seven kids on a farm, that naturally happened, but in today's life, when we are having smaller families, the child seems to become the center of things.

Here was Michael, and I would imagine that since his first Olympics at age fifteen things always revolved around him. People catered to him and his wishes, as he put in the hard work of being an Olympian. People wanted him to succeed and often felt it necessary to put up with his faults, as opposed to correcting them, as they tried to keep him on the Olympic path.

On September 30, 2014, Michael was at a casino and had too much to drink. As he was driving home through a tunnel, he was going eighty-one miles per hour in a fifty-five miles per hour zone and was passing cars in a no-passing zone. He was arrested for driving under the influence with a blood alcohol level of 0.14 percent, when the legal limit was 0.08 percent. In the ESPN video, his coach says he thought that was the final strike against Michael. He was looking back on other times that Michael had gotten in trouble, including a picture that showed up on the internet of him smoking marijuana out of a bong.

After his arrest, Michael went into a depression and locked himself in a room. In the ESPN video, he says that he considered ending his life. All those gold medals couldn't help him get over the mistake of driving drunk. Michael's wife shares in the video that he felt the weight of the world. He felt he was not only letting himself down but all of his fans; he didn't know how he could face them.

Then Ray Lewis, the former NFL football player, entered the picture. He talked Michael through his feelings and gave him a copy of *The Purpose Driven Life*. Michael had always thought of himself as an accident, as his parents were older when they had him. In the book, "Day Two: You Are Not an Accident" told him that was not the case. As he read through the book, he started to focus on the bigger picture. "Day Nineteen: Cultivating Community" told him that relationships are always worth restoring, so he had to reach out to his dad and forgive him. The book helped Michael get his thought life back in focus. He became a dad himself, and he realized he still had contributions to make here on Earth.

It is important that we help our kids find their purpose. **What unique gift did God give them to share with this world?** We all have huge dreams for our kids when they are born. We expect they are going to change the world. The reality is that most kids are going to settle into somewhat of a normal life, but it is important they stay focused on the fact that this normal life includes fulfilling the purpose that God has for them.

I found a great CD from best-selling author and speaker Andy Andrews, who came to Decatur to speak at a Community Leaders Breakfast. As a family, we listened to this CD in the van while we travelled. Andrews is a great story teller. He had one story my kids especially liked about the coach of a baseball team who pronounced the letter "L" as an "R." This coach would tell his team, "Take a rap," meaning "lap." Then one time, he was consoling the kids after a loss, by telling them that it wasn't their fault. Of course, that came out that it wasn't their fart. My kids laughed every time we listened to that story.

Another of Andrews' stories was about the "butterfly effect," the theory that a butterfly could flap its wings and the effects of that movement would be felt across the world. To get the full details, you should look up Andrews' YouTube video on the subject, posted by Michelle Carey, but his point was this: Everything we do has ramifications.

In the video, to illustrate this, Andrews told the story of Norman Borlaug being honored as the ABC News Person of the Week in 2004. Borlaug was one of the originators of corn and wheat modification, which allowed for better production of crops in arid places. As Andrews tells the story, Borlaug joked that he saved two billion people, which certainly should qualify him as Person of the Week, but Andrews asks, what about Henry Wallace? Wallace served as Secretary of Agriculture before becoming Vice President, and he was the one who put Borlaug in charge of the program. If Henry Wallace hadn't done that, maybe the two billion lives wouldn't have been saved, so perhaps Wallace should have been the Person of the Week. However, Wallace came to love agriculture because of a famous student at Iowa State University, where Wallace also attended.

That student's name was George Washington Carver. Maybe Carver should have been Person of the Week? Finally, Andrews talked about Moses and Susan Carver. They were a white couple in Missouri who raised George Washington Carver, after his mother was killed.

Everything you do matters. There are generations yet unborn that your actions may affect.

Wow! That is a lot to think about.

George Washington Carver was a man of both God and science. The two were not separate in his mind. In her article for *The New American*, now on TheFreeLibrary.com, Jodie Gilmore quotes a letter from him, stating:

> How I thank God every day that I can walk and talk with Him. Just last week I was reminded of His omnipotence, majesty and power through a little specimen of mineral sent me for analysis from Bakersfield, California. I have dissolved it, purified it, made conditions favorable for the formation of crystals, when lo before my very eyes, a beautiful bunch of sea green crystals have formed and alongside of them a bunch of snow white ones. Marvel of marvels, how I wish I had you in God's little workshop for a while, how your soul would be lifted up.

Carver viewed his Christian faith as the means by which all the divisions that separate mankind could be transcended. The National Park Service, on his monument's website, quotes him as saying, "We are brothers, all of us, no matter what race or color or condition; children of the same Heavenly Father. We rise together or we fall together." Gilmore notes that Carver viewed his students as his children. She states, "He urged his 'boys' to use nature as a means to coming to know their Creator...." The

National Park Service, in a booklet entitled *Discovering George Washington Carver--A Man of Character*, reprints a letter of Carver's, dated January 9, 1922, in which he listed the "eight cardinal virtues which constitute a lady or a gentleman." These cardinal virtues, which look very similar to my thirteen principles discussed in this book, are:

1st. Be clean both inside and outside.

2nd. Who neither looks up to the rich or down on the poor.

3rd. Who loses, if needs be, without squealing.

4th. Who wins, without bragging.

5th. Who is always considerate of women, children and old people.

6th. Who is too brave to lie.

7th. Who is too generous to cheat.

8th. Who takes his share of the world and lets other people have theirs.

Gilmore notes that, despite a full workload in academia, Carver found time to share his love of Christ:

Carver spent much of his time evangelizing; he wanted to share his love of science and love of God with as many people as possible. He held evening Bible classes at Tuskegee Institute, after he had finished his teaching, research and administrative duties. He was also a leader in the Young Men's Christian Association (YMCA), where he told young people how they could come to understand the mysteries of God by studying nature.

In a couple places in this book, I talk about the opportunity I had to go to Georgia Southern University. It was my dream:

Division I college baseball in the South, replacing Marty Pevey, who became a major leaguer. Who knows how different my life might have been if I had gone? However, I overheard my mom and dad wondering how they were going to come up with the $800 that was needed to get me down there. Because of that, I decided not to go.

If I had gone, perhaps I wouldn't have come home that summer to play Legion ball, which turned out to be one of the best experiences of my life and where many life-long friends were made. The odds are good that I never would have met J. J.'s mother, or at least we wouldn't have had time to date. If I hadn't ended up divorced, I wouldn't have married Suzanne, which led to Kurtis and Emily. Odds are my life would have been completely different had I gone to Georgia Southern. Maybe I would have indeed followed in Marty Pevey's footsteps and made it to the major leagues, but would that have fulfilled God's true purpose for me?

I believe there is a God, and that is the God of the Bible. He has a plan and purpose for our lives. We are not an accident. Things happen for a reason. Sometimes it is really hard to understand that plan when we are going through pain and suffering. Many of the disciples ended up dying horrible deaths. However, I continually remind myself it will all be worth it, if not in this life, then in the next. As we try to sort out life, it is important that we remember that life is preparation for eternity, but we have a purpose here on Earth.

# Life isn't fair! Be a good loser.

*Things turn out best for those who make the best*
*of the way things turn out.--Anonymous*

## Is Life fair?

Did you see the story of Dave Marques in Mount Zion? On the way to a Cardinals game, he stopped in Raymond, Illinois, and on the spur of the moment bought a lottery ticket. He won one million dollars. We contrast that to news at about that same time of a twelve-year-old boy in Mount Pulaski who lost his life in a tragic accident.

In the introduction to this book, I talk about Tom Zobrist, whose son was the World Series MVP. In Principle #7, I write about Jim Collins, whose son was killed by a drunk driver.

Some people will say that there can't be a God, for what God would be this mean, that some people would be so lucky and others would be so unlucky?

I was hit hard by this turn of phrase:

"Life isn't fair--Praise the Lord!"

Eric Altenbernd had just started as Director of Family Ministries at Saint Paul's when I first heard him use this turn of phrase, and it really hit me. Just think how it would be if God gave us what we truly deserve!

We are all sinners who deserve to live apart from God, that is to say, we all deserve hell. However, God loves us and looks past our human failings.

One thing with Kurtis and Emily that just got under my skin was when they argued occasionally about meaningless stuff. I put my foot down early on and said I was not going to have it. I told them, "Sometimes you win; sometimes you lose. Deal with it."

As things went along with the kids, I would talk about whether they were winning or losing. My condolence was, "Sorry you are getting the short end of the stick this time. Maybe next time, we will be able to do what you wanted to do."

Circumstances and money often left me feeling like I wanted to do so much more for my kids than I was able to at the time. In hindsight, it was probably much better for them that I couldn't.

Some people refer to today's kids as the "trophy generation," as in everybody gets a trophy just for participating. One of the great things about sports is that it teaches you how to win and lose. How are you going to respond under pressure? When you have to make big decisions at key points in your life, are you going to be ready? Do you have confidence to bounce back when you make a mistake?

I am not a big fan of going through life as a participant. I can understand that we don't want kids to have a "win at all costs" mentality, but I do think that we want to keep score. Coach Wooden defined success as not trying to be better than someone else, but trying to be the best that you can be. I want kids to learn the value of hard work. I want kids to put in the effort to do their best.

It is very tough to be that kid who has to make the last out of the season. Very few teams get to win their last game of the year, so this happens to most teams. They work the entire year to get to the spot that they are in a meaningful game; then comes the disappointment of losing, but if you don't have spots like that, what is the sense of the hard work? In order to get better and improve and really be your best, there has to be something worthwhile to work for.

"Snowflake" is a term that has come into use today to describe a kid who has a hard time dealing with not getting his or her way. In the WORDview chapter, we shared the story of Opie and the spoiled kid, who certainly qualified as a snowflake.

I remember my mom sharing a story about growing up in Meta, Missouri. We were driving around where she lived as a child, and we stopped to look down a winding lane. Mom reminisced, "As a little girl, I used to walk down this lane to get out to the main road. It was something to do to get away from the house for a little while." I asked, "What did you do after you got here," and she said she just turned around and walked back. When I commented that it didn't sound very exciting, Mom said, "I used to bring my doll along with me. That was my favorite toy. Really, that was my only toy."

I compare that to my grandsons' possessions. They have an entire room of toys: every size basketball possible, trucks and blocks, a tent to hang out in. . . .

I don't tell you this to beat up on my grandkids or the kids who might be considered snowflakes. It is just important that we know what we are working with.

In the Fellowship of Christian Athletes' (FCA) "3Dimensional Coaching" training, they address this issue. "3D" training encourages coaches to not only train kids on the fundamentals or physical parts of a sport, but also to focus on their minds and hearts.

In a flyer promoting 3Dimensional Coaching, the FCA states that "70% of athletes will fail to reach their full potential on & off the field, because of 2nd Dimension [psychological] issues," such as motivation, confidence, emotions, and team cohesion. So many of the strategies we used to learn doing hard work on the farm or growing up as part of a large family just aren't happening any more. Some kids are growing up in two households or have to deal with parents that are not good role models.

As stated in the flyer, the 3D training asks these questions:

**Motivation**--Do you have athletes who will seemingly quit on you in a heartbeat? How do you motivate today's athlete to commit to a long-term process in a culture that values "immediate-gratification?"

**Confidence**--Do you have athletes who shrink back when the game is on the line? How do you help athletes gain/regain confidence in a culture obsessed with publicizing failure?

**Emotions**--Do you have athletes whose emotions get in the way of peak performance? How do you harness the power of passion and emotion in sport to enhance and not hinder athletic ability?

**Team Cohesion**--Do you have athletes who struggle to buy into the team concept? How do you make a team "we" in a culture that constantly sends the message that it's all about "me?"

It's always important to remember that the goal is not to raise good kids, but to raise good adults.

According to an article by Lara Korte, "A new study presented at the Pediatric Academic Societies Meeting in May [2017] found that the number of children and teens admitted to children's hospitals for thoughts of suicide or self-harm have more than doubled during the last decade."

Kids are forced to process a great deal of information these days. They are subject, like we all are, to the twenty-four-hour news cycle. It would seem that some kids have a hard time processing all this information.

What happens when someone takes your parking spot or when someone cuts you off in traffic? If you haven't learned how to lose, you end up with road rage.

But the reality is: Sometimes we win, and sometimes we lose.

In the *Coach Wooden One-on-One* devotional, he talks about "Overcoming Adversity." He starts the chapter off with a quote from James 1:2 MSG: "Consider it a sheer gift, friends, when tests and challenges come at you from all sides."

Wooden goes on to tell the story about how poor his family was when he was growing up. He says, "The pigs got cholera, the drought killed the crops, and we lost the farm, so we moved into town. We still didn't think of it as harsh conditions. It was just necessary. I guess many people who lived through the Great Depression and its aftermath view life that way."

Then he tells the story of when he and his wife were about to get married, and there was a bank failure. He lost $909 that he had saved up in that bank. He had to borrow money to get married.

Wooden finishes with, "The more concerned we become over the things we can't control, the less we will do with the things we can control. My father often quoted Abraham Lincoln on this point: 'We'd all be much happier if we magnified our blessings rather than our disappointments.'"

### Don't you just hate it when your kid is hurt?

Doesn't it feel like good parenting when you stick that pacifier in the baby's mouth, and the baby stops crying?

How about when that terrible teacher tells your kid that he is not learning at the pace that he should? Maybe he should spend a little less time on the video games and a little more time on his studies. Doesn't it feel great to call that teacher and stand up for your child?

These days, many people do just that. Some parents can be heard to say, "How dare you try to criticize my child!"

At some point, we have to let our kids go through some pain.

How do we get stronger physically? By lifting weights. How do we get stronger mentally? We need to do some weight lifting in this area as well. If we solve our children's problems for them, they never build up this mental strength.

In the book *A Gameplan for Life: The Power of Mentoring*, by John Wooden and Don Yaeger, I love John Wooden's discussion about how Abraham Lincoln faced adversity:

> One of the first things that stood out to me about Lincoln's life was the way he handled adversity. His mother died while he was still very young. He didn't have consistent access to schooling, so he taught himself. He was defeated in his first attempt at public office. He filed for bankruptcy. He was unlucky in love. He lost three times in his bid for the U.S. Senate. He suffered from what would probably be considered by today's standards to be severe clinical depression. But he persevered. It wasn't just his presidency that interested me; it was also everything he encountered on the road to the presidency that really captured my attention.
>
> Had Lincoln been given the option, he probably would not have selected all of the trials he suffered; but rather than collapsing under their weight, he used them to strengthen himself for his next goal. He was determined to learn from everything that came his way, even if the lesson was painful and the experience heartbreaking. "I do not think much of a man who is not wiser today than he was yesterday," he once remarked. To him, life was a series of lessons that presented opportunities. Wisdom came from making the most of each one.

It seems to me that had Lincoln not gone through all of the disappointments he did before he became the commander in chief, he would not have been adequately prepared to preside during arguably the most tumultuous period of American history. Because he had not been spared the harsh realities of life--the heartaches and the disappointments--he could deal with the larger trials that awaited him down the road.

Lincoln himself once said, "The worst things you can do for those you love are the things they could and should do for themselves." He fiercely believed in self-sufficiency, and in the maturity and character that struggles and hardships can bring. This lesson is so important for teachers and parents. It is only natural for us to want to shield our students and our children from anything that might possibly cause them hurt or to suffer or even to be uncomfortable. But some degree of pain is necessary for a person to become suited for the responsibilities that lay ahead.

As we remember 9/11 and see other tragedies around the world, we hear the question asked, "Where is God?"

I ask again: How do you get strong physically? By lifting weights. How do you get stronger mentally and spiritually? By handling the weights of a life that doesn't always go as expected.

At my mom's funeral, Pastor Wray preached on Luke 23:43 ESV, where Jesus tells the repentant sinner on the cross, "Today you will be with me in Paradise." I believe that my mom and the others who profess Christ are in a Heaven that is a Paradise. We don't earn our way to Heaven; it is a free gift of God through His grace. However, we do have to stay committed to the team.

Sometimes, it's hard to understand what the coach is trying

to do or what God's plan is. However, I believe that God does have a plan. My human mind can't explain an event like 9/11 or how someone as faithful as Rachel Scott was the first to die at Columbine. (For a moving description of Rachel's faith, see Judy Tarjanyi's article, "Columbine victim's dad traveling to share his daughter's journal," published in the *Toledo Blade*.) However, it helps me to realize that life is God's test for us. If we stay committed to the team, God will reveal His glory in Heaven.

The global Christian ministry Focus on the Family recently posted a devotion that has a similar viewpoint:

> Job was a "blameless and upright man" (Job 1:1 [NIV, paraphrased]). In spite of this, he experienced terrible sufferings. He lost seven sons, three daughters, and all his property in a single day. After that, he was deprived of his health and his self-respect. It all came about simply because Satan thought it would be interesting to see how he'd respond. *And God allowed it to happen.*
>
> Was that fair? Was it just, loving, and kind of the Creator to stand aside and let this avalanche of tragedy and pain come crashing down on the head of a good man? . . .
>
> The remarkable thing [the thing we need to remember whenever we find ourselves in Job's position] is that the question never receives a direct answer. In fact, when God finally speaks to Job out of the whirlwind (Job 38:1), He treats the question as if it's beside the point. Justice is not the issue, He seems to say. Life in a fallen world can never be "fair." . . .
>
> In the final analysis, God does not resolve the problem of unjust human suffering by

*explaining* it. Instead, He *enters into it.* In the person of Jesus Christ He experiences what it is like to be unfairly accused, arrested, tried, condemned, beaten, reviled, spit upon and put to death. An innocent man, He bears the penalty while Barabbas, a criminal and an assassin, goes free. He takes upon Himself the burden of our anguish and pain. He drinks the cup to its dregs. He does not murmur or complain. In so doing, He demonstrates His love for us and sends us this unmistakable message: the answer [to the problem of suffering] . . . can't be discovered by means of theological rationalization. The answer [to the problem] . . . is *Jesus* [italics in original].

**"Uncoachable kids become unemployable adults. Let your kid get used to somebody being tough on them! That's life, get over it."--Kevin Boley, Head Boys Basketball Coach, Legend Titans**

Sometimes you win--Sometimes you learn.--John C. Maxwell

As we transition to the next chapter about winning, I would like to take a few minutes and tell you about one of the more interesting times of my life. This was when I was able to play fastpitch softball, including with the Decatur Pride. I was a part of over 500 wins with the Pride. On average, we played 100 games a year. During this time frame, I learned a great deal about winning and losing.

The Pride was expected to win. In the 1991-1996 timeframe, budgets ran around $200,000 to $350,000 per year. We brought in pitchers from New Zealand and flew in top players from all around the country. When you spend that amount of money, there definitely was pressure to "get it done." We also played in front of some nice-sized crowds. I have a picture taken by Lori Ann Cook that appeared in the Bloomington *Pantagraph* on September 14, 1992; in the caption, it was estimated there were 6,000 people in attendance that day. One year we traveled to Canada to play a game against the Toronto Gators. They were considered Canada's best team, while we were considered the best USA team. The crowd at that game was estimated to be around 5,000.

One of my favorite turns of phrase that developed while playing softball was, "How we gonna win it?" In an effort to maintain a confident outlook and focus on the positive, the question wasn't whether or not we would win; it was only how we were going to do it.

When my son J. J. was twelve, I was the coach for his baseball team, and we adopted this philosophy. One of the guys on the team, Brit Miller, went on to star as a linebacker for the University of Illinois Fighting Illini and then played in the NFL with the San Francisco Giants and the Saint Louis Rams. I get goose bumps when I run into Brit these days and he says, "Hey coach, how we gonna win it!"

On the occasion that a Pride team got behind, we always had the goal of cutting the lead in half. How do you eat an elephant? One bite at a time, same way that you eat anything else. Instead of feeling like we were facing an insurmountable lead, we would cut it down into bite-size pieces.

My brother Rick was a tremendous competitor. It was such an honor to get to play with him. In 2017, he was inducted into the Amateur Softball Association (ASA)/Team USA National Softball Hall of Fame. He went in with University of Arizona softball coach Mike Candrea, whose teams were eight-time NCAA National Champions and won Olympic gold and silver medals. Olympian and pro All-Star Jennie Finch was inducted the year before.

This is a speech that I gave when Rick was inducted into the Illinois ASA Hall of Fame in 2013:

Rick Minton played softball for almost twenty-seven years, starting in 1981 with Herbert Trucking and finishing playing "A" ball in Cerro Gordo. It is a great honor for Rick to be inducted into the Illinois ASA Hall of Fame, but I really believe that he deserves to represent Illinois, and especially Decatur, in the national ASA hall of fame.

The first "C" that I would use to describe Rick is Competitor. It didn't matter if it was the Pan American games or Wednesday night in Cerro Gordo--Rick showed up to compete. He started as a pinch runner and outfielder, and finished as arguably the best second baseman in the history of the game.

I remember one year after Shelbyville High School won the state basketball championship, we honored them out at Borg Warner Field. We had some shirts printed up that said, "Shelbyville Basketball and Decatur Pride Softball--Winning is our business, and business is good!" I think that phrase really describes Rick.

My tally says that Rick was part of more than 1,500 wins for Decatur softball. [Herald & Review sportswriter] Mark Tupper wrote a letter for Rick's nomination and stated, "Always in top condition, always up for the big games, always healthy and in the lineup, Rick Minton was in many ways the heart and soul of those great Decatur teams. Those teams had other ASA Hall of Fame caliber players like Rothrock, Hicks, Place and Scott, but it was Rick who kept them playing fast and loose."

The second "C" I would use is Character. I am using that term in a Babe Ruth or Harry Caray sort of way. How many people do you know that go by the nickname of "Bonehead" and *like* it? Tupper called Rick the "soundtrack" of Decatur Softball. It took an awful lot of money to play softball Decatur style, so it not only needed to be a game, it needed to be a show. Rick played with flair; people showed up and paid their money because they wanted to see what Rick might do. Sometimes it was having a heated discussion with [umpire]Ron Runyon over the proper application of the strike zone, but sometimes it was hitting the dramatic home run.

In Tupper's letter, he said that Rick "was a defensive magician. He could make all the routine plays, but he would routinely make all the difficult plays. Again, it didn't matter whether it was under the biggest lights or the worst lights - you always knew you were going to get your best from Rick. He truly loved to play the game."

It always amazed me though, how as soon as the game was over, it was over. Guys that Rick was in a knock-down, drag-out fight with twenty minutes ago were buying the first round for him. Long-time teammate Brent Stevenson said, "I traveled and played the game at the highest level with Rick, and I can tell you he was respected and liked by everyone. It was war between the lines and then great friendship off the field."

Finally, the last "C" is for Champion: 1984 International Softball Congress World Champion, 1988 gold medalist, playing for the USA in the International Softball Federation Worlds, 1994 and 1995 ASA National Championships, you can even throw in a couple of over-forty National

Championships. Rick has six silver medals from U.S. National Sports Festivals and Pan American Games. He played in Pan Am Games in Cuba and Argentina.

I remember the 1987 Pan Am Games in Indianapolis. It was right after his son Ryan was born, so Rick was driving back and forth to Indy every day to play. I rode over with him once and saw that this team of the best players in the U.S. had Rick batting cleanup that day.

Dave Boys also wrote a letter to the committee for Rick. Now, Dave wasn't too bad of a player; he played on some decent teams, with some above average teammates . . . of course, I am playing this down. You have more rings than fingers, right, Dave? Dave said, "I honestly think Rick Minton is the best big-game player I have ever played with."

Tupper also noted in his letter that Rick not only thrived in the ASA Men's Major game, but he also helped USA Softball as well. To this day, Rick is recognized throughout the United States, Canada and New Zealand as a legend of the game.

So the final "C," Rick, is "Congrats." Momma Minton would be proud.

I learned so much from Rick about going out and giving it your best. As shown in *My Personal Best*, John Wooden puts "Competitive Greatness" at the top of his Pyramid of Success. If you really want to separate the men from the boys, as they say, you have to be at your best when your best is required. Very few are capable of doing that. In this small way, I was so blessed to be able to learn some of these things from my brother.

Back in the fastpitch softball days, each year we hosted the Herald & Review Decatur Shootout, which brought teams to Decatur from all over the country. The worst thing you could do in this event was to get in the losers' bracket, because then you knew you were going to have to play a bunch more games to win. Again, though, how do you eat that elephant? One bite at a time.

Over my time with the Pride, we suffered some really tough losses as well. I have a vivid memory from the 1991 International Softball Congress World Tournament. I had called for Brent Stevenson to throw a high rise ball to get the batter, Gary Fransen from the Midland Michigan Explorers, to pop up the bunt that we were expecting him to lay down. Pop it up he did; I will always remember the sound of that softball tinging off the scoreboard, but Gary didn't bunt. He swung away and hit a game winning homer. Oops!

I mentioned our game in Toronto. It was a great pitchers' duel between Chubb Tangeroa and Darren Zack, two of the greatest pitchers to ever take the mound, in front of the big crowd, that is until a routine fly ball was hit to me in left field. Most of my life I was a catcher, but my knees had started giving me some trouble. I spent some time at first base, but other times they would try to hide me in left field. On this particular night, I was not up to the task. My excuse was the fact that the lighting wasn't very good, but the fact of the matter was I dropped an ordinary fly ball that cost us the game.

Here this big crowd had showed up to see the two greatest teams in North America, and what they got was a guy who couldn't catch a simple fly ball.

But the great thing about Decatur Pride softball was that there was always tomorrow. The very next day, we played in the Perth Shootout. This was one of the biggest and most prestigious softball tournaments in the world. The best teams from Canada were there, along with some of the best United States squads. I hit the ball well throughout our Canadian trip, but in the Perth shootout, I actually managed to make a game winning catch in the outfield as well.

A line drive was hit deep to left field. I was going as fast as I could go, at a full sprint. At this point in my career, I wasn't the fastest guy, but I was giving it everything I had. I reached over the fence, and at the same time, I slammed *into* the fence. I felt like it cut me in half as I doubled over it. When I came back up, the wind was out of me, but the softball was in my glove. I had robbed a home run to save the game.

It's important in life to have a bounce-back attitude. **It has been said that success is going from failure to failure without a loss of enthusiasm.**

I am blessed to have a video of a hit that I got off of Marty Pienick in the 1993 ASA National Championship game. While the hit did break up his perfect game, we were down 6-0 at the time, and we ended up losing by that score. However, that loss paved the way to the national championship rings that we won in 1994 and 1995.

Lots of great people were losers before they were winners. Michael Jordan was cut from his high school basketball team. How many attempts did Thomas Edison make at the light bulb before he actually got it right?

Life has a lot of disappointment. It's important that we learn how to deal with it.

# Life isn't fair! Be a good winner.

*Sometimes you win. Sometimes you lose.*
*Talent is God-given; be humble.*
*Fame is man-given; be thankful.*
*Conceit is self-given; be careful.*
*--John Wooden (from My Personal Best)*

## How do you handle success?

I love the movie *Bull Durham*. (Make sure you get the TV version though, and even then, many of the topics are of an adult nature.) I am a baseball guy, and there is a great deal of baseball humor in the movie. It is also an interesting perspective on taking talent and putting it together with knowledge. In one scene, veteran ballplayer Crash teaches the rookie Nuke about the usefulness of clichés. Crash gives a whole list of helpful expressions, such as: We have to play them one day at a time. I am just happy to be here. I hope I can help the ball club. I just want to give it my best shot, and, the good Lord willing, things will work out.

If you ever have a chance to do an interview, you can use some of the phrases from *Bull Durham*, although hopefully with more sincerity. Anything that is humble and thankful and complimentary of others is a good approach. If it is appropriate, give thanks to God, saying things like, "I have been blessed to stay healthy and have a good season." Thank your teammates with, "Any success that I have had is because of them." Thank your coach, who has really helped you develop. Praise your opponents for being tough competition that required you to play your best.

There is no better example of this than Trevor Bayne's interview after he won the 2011 Daytona 500, which I'll talk about later on.

Unfortunately, there are lots of examples of athletes who didn't use this approach. One of them was Terrel Owens, or "T. O.," as he preferred to be called. He was arguably one of the best wide receivers ever to play football. Just ask him; he'll tell you.

Sometimes it is hard to stay humble in athletics, because confidence does play a big part in performance. If you are going to play sports at the highest level, you have to really, really believe in yourself, but as a good winner, you have to try to keep that ego on the inside.

I remember when T. O. caught a touchdown pass against Dallas and then ran to the middle of the field to stand in the center of their star. When he played with the Philadelphia Eagles, he once took a shot at his own quarterback, Donavan McNabb. T. O. was often known for imitating the touchdown dances of players on the opposing team. One of his favorite lines was, "I love me some me."

There is a saying that when a professional football player scores a touchdown, he should act like he has been there before. T. O. always took the World Wrestling Federation approach, which might sell some tickets, but I don't like what it teaches our kids.

Look up an interview with football player Apollos Hester on YouTube. His postgame remarks are a combination of T. O. and of doing things the right way.

The Pride taught me a lot about being a good winner.

I think I am safe in saying that it was a thrill for a lot of teams to play us on a Wednesday night. These mid-week games usually involved us taking on one of the local teams. Fastpitch softball was a big deal in the 1990s, before a variety of factors ran the game into the ground. (I made a small appearance in a movie entitled *Fastpitch*, which talks about the popularity of the game at the time and how it was fading fast.)

We were blessed to play our home games at Borg Warner Field, which was a very nice facility that gave you a bit of a minor league ballgame feel. "Earthmover Credit Union Night" was always extra special, as it brought out the Caterpillar employees and provided a festive atmosphere. It was a highlight of many teams' seasons to come play against the best in such a nice atmosphere, but after all the pregame excitement, it wasn't uncommon for us to score five or six runs in the first inning. The game would be over about as quickly as it started. Now what do you do? We never wanted to win a game 20-0, but fans showed up and paid their money to see the game.

Terry Wiebe was a guy who came down from Canada to play with us. He was one of the all-time great competitors and served as the shortstop on the Canadian National Team. He won a variety of Pan American Games and International Softball Federation (ISF) World Championships gold medals playing for his country and was part of our 1994 ASA National Championship in Decatur. He was also good at hitting into double plays on purpose.

When we were up by a comfortable score, Terry would always take one for the team. He wasn't afraid to gracefully strike out. He was so good; if he came up with a runner on first, he could guide a ground ball to the shortstop, who could step on the bag and throw to first for the double play. Terry's batting average was always towards the top of the team, but it would have been even higher if you could have factored out the times that he made outs on purpose.

I hope the past few paragraphs came across the right way. We always wanted to have respect for the guys who loved the game. We knew that the small-town teams from places like Nokomis, Teutopolis and Pickneyville were part of what made fastpitch softball so great, but these teams weren't designed to compete at our level.

We lost a few Wednesday night games when we didn't show up to play our best or when the other teams had exceptionally good nights. Teams from Taylorville always seemed to give the Pride a good battle. For two years, I was part of the T-ville Max Klemm bunch before getting to move on. The Pride was just so good because it was a team that was constructed of the best players from the other teams in the area. Plus, we brought in guys like Wiebe and first-rate pitchers from New Zealand. Therefore, some games were not on a level playing field, and it was up to us to be good winners and respect the game.

Sometimes, it is really hard to figure out what is the right or wrong approach. In the following scenario, I'm not quite sure if I took the right approach. To this day, I continue to play it out in my head.

In 2009, I was helping to coach Kurtis' team, the Champaign Tribe. Our season ended with a loss in the Continental Amateur Baseball Association (CABA) World Series in Tennessee.

This Tribe team was loaded with talent. Many of the kids went on to play college sports. Illini basketball player Michael Finke was our three-hitter and first baseman. At age fourteen, Mike was around six foot, four inches tall and only weighed about 140 pounds, but he was such a great athlete. Ross Learnard and Nick Stokowski were good players at Parkland College, before going Division I. Ross went on to be an All-American at Purdue, posting the lowest earned run average (ERA) in the history of the school. Hunter Morris played at Eastern Illinois University. Ross Hutchinson was a very good player at Illinois State. As of this 2017 writing, any of these guys still might have a shot at playing professionally.

When we gathered after the team lost their last game and

the season was over, I told them that I was disappointed in them, that I didn't think they lived up to their potential. This team had the ability to do some very special things, but we never quite got over the hump. At the time, these fourteen-year-olds had a lot on their plates. One of our better pitchers, Kyle Brazas, would go on to be a good quarterback for his high school football team. He had been practicing for that, as well as playing baseball. Of course, Finke always had basketball on his mind. On multiple occasions, these kids played a double header in Midwest heat, and there would still be a serious basketball game at the hotel that evening. It was my opinion that baseball wasn't always the highest priority for these kids.

I struggle sometimes with the discussions about coaches preferring multi-sport athletes. It is my opinion that the sooner you can figure out what you want to be good at, the better off you are going to be. Tiger Woods knew at a young age what he wanted to do in life. On the other side, maybe that is why his career got cut a little bit short. When Wayne Gretzky was ten years old, they were already calling him "the Great One." Venus and Serena Williams started gaining fame and focusing only on tennis at the age of twelve. Michael Phelps made his first Olympics at fifteen. Lebron James knew his future at a very young age.

Sometimes when you are in the middle of something, you don't realize just how special it is, but I knew those two years with the Champaign Tribe were pretty amazing. These were some of the most special kids you could ever put together, and it was such a blessing for Kurtis to be able to play with them. I have really enjoyed following their careers. But at the end of that World Series, I didn't think they had lived up to their potential in that particular season, and I felt that they were big enough boys to hear the honest truth.

God has given us all unique abilities. Another John Wooden saying that came from his father, recorded in *Coach Wooden*

*One-on-One*, was, "Never try to be better than somebody else. Always learn from others and never cease trying to be the best you can be." I told the boys that it is essential to focus on the task at hand, and I felt like their minds were often elsewhere during the season. It was great, but it could have been better.

I sure hope that I wasn't too hard on the kids, but I didn't see any of those guys as snowflakes. They have proven me correct with their accomplishments since that year.

Trevor Bayne would certainly fall into that category of figuring out early in life what he was going to focus on. At the age of five, his family discovered that he was really good at going fast in vehicles. At fifteen, he moved away from his parents to North Carolina to pursue a career in racing. He had enough success that he was running around in his own H2 Hummer, but his parents had done a good job of establishing a firm foundation. Despite a wreck in that vehicle that could've done him serious harm, he had a good head on his shoulders and a firm relationship with Jesus.

I get goosebumps every time I watch the video recap of Trevor winning the 2011 Daytona 500.

Trevor had worked his way up to a place in this Super Bowl of stock car racing and was getting a lot of pre-race love from some of the big names of the sport. NASCAR had tried to change a few things up that year with restrictor plates, and it created a situation where two cars could go much faster than one. Trevor had worked successfully with Jeff Gordon in some of the pre-races, since Trevor excelled at being the push car in the two-car tandem. When it came time for the major event, he was thrilled that his hero, Jeff Gordon, wanted to work with him during the race.

As Trevor's car rolled around the track waiting for the race to begin, Darrell Waltrip decided to call on him for an interview. It caught Trevor in the middle of a prayer. It is always a good time to pray, but I guess it is especially good when you are about to drive a racecar at 200 miles per hour. What a witness for this prayer to go out on national TV! Trevor gave you the feeling it was going to be a special day.

The race started as expected, with Trevor pushing Gordon around the track. Then, only thirty-five laps in, Gordon ran into the back of another car and had to go to the back of the pack. Trevor had to come up with a new game plan.

There was a major wreck that took out a lot of the favorites in the race, but Trevor was able to avoid it. Finally, he found another partner to work with in David Reagan. Then, after one more wreck, Trevor found himself as the leader of the Daytona 500. He had spent the entire race pushing other cars; now, he was at the front.

With two laps to go, the goosebumps start. Could this rookie, on the day of his twentieth birthday, really win the Daytona 500?

Bobby LaBonte gave Trevor the push he needed to get out front. However, in this sort of racing, the leader is usually a sitting duck. Because of drafting, it is hard for the leader to stay in the lead.

With one lap to go, the white flag waved; Trevor was still leading. As Carl Edwards came up to pass him on the final stretch, Trevor dropped down in front of him and was able to take the checkered flag. In his first Daytona 500, while celebrating his twentieth birthday, he accomplished his childhood dream. "Are you kidding me," he screamed on the radio. He followed that up with, "God is so good!"

If you go to "NASCARAllOut" on YouTube and look up the 2011 Daytona 500, you should find about a thirty-minute video that is an awesome example of how to be successful at winning.

When we are successful, our human sinful nature is for us to take the credit: "Yeah, *I* did that. Look at me!" We have all seen examples of pro athletes who didn't handle their moment in the sun very well.

NASCAR drivers are often the kings of cliché, with rehearsed lines stored in their heads and ready to use at a moment's notice. After all, it is part of the job to thank the sponsors any time a driver gets a chance, but would Trevor really have had something prepared for what to do if he was the winner? After all, he was just the push car driver in only his first race. You can bet all his post-race remarks were genuinely from the heart.

As you can see in a YouTube video posted by SlicedSmoke14, when Trevor got to the winner's circle, he handled his victory with incredible grace. As he got out of his car, with confetti flying everywhere and people screaming, he pointed to the sky. A reporter started with, "Every young kid who has ever stepped into a race car has dreamt of this moment," and then called him Travis. In a very humble tone, Trevor said, "We said a prayer before, you know we pray a lot and we expect a lot of things, but this just shows how powerful God is." He pointed to his teammates and continued, "I am so thankful for the job these guys did. . . . Our first 500, are you kidding me? . . . I can't thank these guys that worked with me all day enough. There were ten, fifteen different drivers that pushed us. Carl helped us to get across the [finish] line. I don't know what happened with David [Reagan] there at that one point. . . . Wow! This is unbelievable!" He went on to thank many others, including his fans.

In the biggest race of his life, Trevor had prepared to do his best and ended up being the winner. After the race, he was just as big a winner in the way that he glorified God.

In a video on the website IAmSecond.com, Trevor tells a story about losing focus on God as his career hit a speed bump, but when he turned his racing back over to God, amazing things happened. What an incredible example of how to handle success!

Another great example of being a good winner is Tim Tebow. Tim is the son of a missionary. He is very genuine in his faith.

The saying that I always attribute to Tim is, "Work as if everything depended on you; pray as if everything depended on

God." It was actually Saint Ignatius of Loyola who said it first, but Tim has done an awesome job of living up to it.

On Tim's website, it says, "True success is not measured in physical possessions, but in the amount of lives that you change." One of his biggest successes of late is his Night to Shine program. He lays out a blueprint for churches and organizations throughout the country to put on a prom for those who normally wouldn't get to go.

The Tim Tebow Foundation's website describes this event as follows:

An unforgettable prom night experience, centered on God's love, for people with special needs ages 14 and older. . . . Night to Shine celebrates the uniqueness of each individual guest, by providing an unforgettable night where they are welcomed, valued and loved! . . . On one night, February 9, 2018, 537 churches from around the world came together to host 90,000 honored guests through the support of 175,000 volunteers.

If you search on Tim Tebow on YouTube, you will find a couple of videos where he is miked up in an NFL game. It is amazing to watch and listen to him work. He is a fierce competitor who loves the Lord.

In his book *Shaken*, Tebow shares his WORDview with the quote, "My identity is based on belonging to God. No one can take this foundation away from me." Following are some other quotes from Tim that tie in very well with my 13 principles.

Principle # 2
"Regardless of how your life will impact others and what that will look like, I just know that when your identity is grounded in God, when you trust in him, you become part of a bigger picture. And you begin to live out this wonderful poem he has written for your life. This is the truth when

life is smooth sailing, and this is the truth when storms come." (from *Shaken*)

"God created each of us special, each with gifts and abilities like no one else's. He created each of us different, fully intending that we would use our unique gifts and abilities to do what He created us to do." (from *Through My Eyes*)

"You and I were created by God to be so much more than normal. . . . Following the crowd is not a winning approach in life. In the end it's a loser's game, because we never become who God created us to be by trying to be like everybody else." (from *Through My Eyes*)

Principles # 3 & 4
"No matter what, win or lose, Lord give me the strength to honor You."
(prayer during December 11, 2011, NFL game versus the Chicago Bears)

"Regardless of what happens, I still honor my Lord and Savior Jesus Christ, because at the end of the day, that's what's important, win or lose." (interview, Easter Sunday 2012, Celebration Church, Georgetown, Texas, quoted by Jim Denison)

Principle #5
"And that's the great thing about living the Christian life and trying to live by faith, that you're trying to get better every day. You're trying to improve."
(interview, *The O'Reilly Factor*, June 3, 2011)

"Hard work beats talent, when talent doesn't work hard."
(Tim Tebow quoting Tim Notke, quoted by Mike Yorkie in *Playing with Purpose*)

Principle #7
"I made a conscious choice not to give up, not to gripe, not to pout, not to let others define me."
(from *Shaken*)

"You know what I've learned in the process? How important it is not to allow either the highs or the lows in life to determine who you are." (from *Shaken*)

Principle #8
"If you want to be great in the Kingdom of God, it's pretty clear--humble yourself and serve those around you, and you will be great."
(interview, University of Mobile Leadership Banquet, April 18, 2013, quoted by Mark Inabinett)

I am not sure who to credit this to, but I will close with this: Cooperate with others. Compete against yourself.

# Develop good habits.

*The father of a righteous child has great joy; a*
*man who fathers a wise son rejoices in him.*
*--Proverbs 23:24 NIV*

The goal as a parent is for things to get easier.

I remember my little dog, Toby. For the first four years, I gladly would have given this dog away, before we finally settled into a rhythm, and he became a big part of our family.

The same thing should happen with your kids. As a kid grows, you go from one set of struggles to another, but I believe these simple principles apply to all the stages of child-rearing. Once you can get your kid trained in how to think and approach things, communication is much easier, and the rough patches aren't quite as rough. If you can get your kids into this rhythm, there is a lot more harmony to your life.

As a five foot, eleven inch, 230-pound person, I am not sure that I have any room to talk about establishing good habits. My food habits could be a great deal better. I once heard a wise man ask, "Do you live to eat or eat to live?" I would love to tell you that I am the latter, but earlier in the book I said, "Don't lie."

I am blessed that I have never been a fan of coffee, so I don't have the habit of drinking it all day. However, I do like to have a glass of iced tea in the morning. When I was thirty-five, I was in the Wagon Restaurant drinking a beer, and suddenly my face felt as if it was on fire, like I was having some sort of reaction to the beer. I guess that was God's way of telling me it was time to give up the alcohol. (About once a year, I will make sure that I still have the same reaction, and yes, my face still gets flushed.) For several years, I got away from drinking pop, but that habit has crept back in.

Many years ago, I bought some self-help tapes from Anthony "Tony" Robbins. One of the principles was: What do you associate with pain, and what do you associate with pleasure? When you look at a piece of chocolate cake, is that painful, or is that pleasurable? My take-away from the tapes was that you have to find a way to associate pain with things that you don't want in your life and pleasure with those that you do.

If you look at the instance above with alcohol, you see where that naturally happened for me. Drinking a beer became painful, so I quit doing it.

I had another instance with cigars. When my brother played in the Pan American Games in Cuba, he came home with some of the renowned Cuban cigars. He brought them to Sioux City, Iowa, where we were playing in a softball tournament. We were having a few drinks and a bite to eat, when I decided I would see what all the fuss was about Cuban cigars.

In a short period of time, I was dizzy, and the next thing you know, I was losing my dinner. Now, whenever I get anywhere close to a cigar, Cuban or not, it about makes me sick. This one event put cigars into my "painful" category.

We have to try to do the same things with our kids, not to give them Cuban cigars but to get them to associate pain with behavior that we don't want and pleasure with behavior that we do want.

Don't be surprised if your kids associate pleasure with what you do. If you're a Cub or Cardinal fan, they are likely to do the same, so be careful what you enjoy in front of your kids. A lot of what we teach kids is caught not taught.

*"Children have never been very good at listening to their elders,*
*but they have never failed to imitate them."--James Baldwin*

I have always seen Oreos as a great metaphor for sin. Does anybody eat regular Oreos? If you are going to go ahead and give in to temptation, you might as well go for the Double Stuf Oreos. Let's be honest: Sin is often pleasurable in the short run. We are all going to grab an Oreo here and there, but what happens when we sit down and eat the entire package? What happens when we sit down and eat an entire package every day? We may get away with it for a period of time, but at some point, it is going to catch up with us.

Proverbs 14:12 NIV says, "There is a way that appears to be right, but in the end it leads to death."

As I look at our culture today, it seems that we are only focused on the pleasures of eating Oreos and not the side effects. We celebrate the ghetto lifestyle with hip hop music. You are labeled a hater if you don't embrace alternative life styles and speak out for the traditional family structure. We watch reality shows where one guy is with twenty girls. Pastor Wray recently shared in an amazing sermon, "Right and wrong has become a movable target because it is no longer founded on God's word."

Johnny was in Sunday school, and the teacher asked him what he knew about the Resurrection. "I know that if it lasts more than four hours, you should call the doctor."

This would be funny if it weren't so true. Many of our kids know more about erectile dysfunction than they do about the Resurrection of Jesus.

I have always tried to point out to my kids that nothing good happens after 11:00 p.m. Any time there is an accident that occurs after 11:00 p.m., I try to let my kids know about it. I've heard it said that one out of every four drivers on the road after 11:00 has been drinking. Many of the articles will say that so-and-so died in a car accident on Sunday morning. The headline gives you the impression that they were on their way to church when it happened, but a little research reveals that it occurred in the very early morning hours, like at 2:00 a.m. When it came time for my kids to be out with their friends on their own, when do you think their curfew was?

What is your normal daily routine? In 2017, I attended my grandson Eli's dedication, and the pastor talked about this concept of getting into a rhythm. You need to get into a rhythm of taking care of your responsibilities, including work, family time, learning, exercise and making sure that God is part of your day.

Some kids get into the habit of video games. According to his *Leadership Game Plan for Success*, another John Wooden saying is, "Practice moderation and balance in all that you do." Parents need to help kids practice moderation in this area. A good approach might be, "Get your homework done, and you can have an hour. Get your chores done, and you can have another hour." This goes back to Kevin Leman's Reality Discipline that I talked about in Principle #1.

Video games are very addictive. There are a few positives, such as they get kids to strive for the next level. Tony Robbins has another little nugget of wisdom with his acronym CANI, which stands for Constant And Never-ending Improvement. Point out to kids that when they are playing video games, they are doing this. They want to get to the next level; they want a higher score. Tell them it is a good thing to compete against themselves to try to get better, but you also have to point out that very few kids can support themselves playing video games. Say something like, "You need to keep this in moderation and make sure that you take time for other activities that have other benefits. Working at a sport that involves exercise gives you some health benefits. Homework can prepare you for opportunities down the road to get a job."

In an article for BreakPoint, John Stonestreet and G. Shane Morris recently posted about this, saying:

If there is a stereotype that lives up to reality these days, it's the unemployed, disaffected, twenty-something American male who haunts his parents' basement, addicted to World of Warcraft. In the year 2000, 35 percent of young men without bachelor's degrees lived in their parents' homes. Today a majority do, and among the unemployed, that number is a staggering 70 percent. According to University of Chicago economist Erik Hurst, these men are spending the overwhelming bulk of their time playing video games.

The article then finishes up with, "One of the most important things parents can give their children, especially young men, are boundaries when it comes to games and distractions. But even more important, a sense of their God-given calling to actively engage the world around them. Pick up a copy of "A Practical Guide to Culture" by visiting our website, BreakPoint.org."

How about good eating habits? I remember being told by a parent that her child only eats chicken fingers. (I never knew that chickens had fingers.) I feel like my parents when I say, "You will eat what I cook, or you won't eat." Kids should not dictate to parents. It's one thing to offer your child a choice between hot dogs and mac and cheese, but be very careful that they don't start getting focused on a limited diet that has them eating only their personal favorites.

You have to make sure that you kick the kid out of the house once in a while for some exercise. Maybe it's just a walk. Maybe it's Pokémon Go. Kids have got to get used to exercise, though, or it is going to come back to get them in the long run.

Todd Tuggle, a local pastor, recently podcast a sermon about the Sabbath. He did a great job of emphasizing the need we have to mix in a day of rest. Even God rested on the seventh day. As we follow God's plan, it's good to take some time to rest.

One of the habits that I think we need to get into is **that of being a good listener**. I love to use a picture of a basset hound with his giant floppy ears held up in attention to make this point.

Proverbs 18:13 NIV says, "To answer before listening--that is folly and shame."

I'm not sure who gets the credit for the saying that God gave you two ears and one mouth, so use them in that proportion.

When I am listening, I am learning!

People don't care how much you know until they know how much you care, and one of the number one ways to show people that you care is to listen.

Many people only listen in order to respond. As soon as they have decided what they're going to say back, they quit listening. When you listen to understand, you hear the person out.

For part of my life, I wasn't much of a communicator. I was the typical guy: Ask me a question, and I will usually answer your question, but not a great deal more.

However, as I thought about wanting to be a better conversationalist, I realized my wife was a great example. She was very good at talking to seniors. She was also very good at talking on the phone for a long time, but we will focus on the positives. (I'm joking, of course.) What was her secret? She would ask one more question. When people told her something, she would ask a question to continue the subject and go deeper. As a journalism major, I should've known that. Over my lifetime, I have done a wide variety of radio work. I know that the key to doing a good job on the radio is to ask good questions and keep people talking, yet I didn't seem to do that in my regular conversations.

As I worked on becoming a more valuable person, I ran into in some information from pastor and author Josh Hunt. Josh likes to work with people who like to teach the Bible. As he looks at some of the concerns that are in the church, he recommends that the people who are teaching the Bible ask better questions.

As I have led a Thursday morning men's group, I have tried to focus on asking good questions that really make people think. When most people think of a salesman, they think of a good talker. However, if a salesman is really doing a good job of providing solutions to his customer's problems, he will do a lot of listening before he talks or recommends a specific product. In my work as a financial advisor, I use the joke that the difference between a doctor and a drug dealer is that a doctor will ask you a few questions before recommending that you buy some drugs.

As I watch politics today, I see a lot of kids that are demanding things. **One of the best things we can do for our kids is to teach them to be good listeners.**

When I go to lunch with someone, I like to pay attention to who gets done eating first. Obviously other things can affect this, but usually the person that has done the most listening will finish their food first.

If I feel like I've been dominating the conversation, I always try to stop myself and come up with a question to ask the other party. Most people are not that good as listeners, and if you have talked for a long time, they have probably started to tune you out anyway. There are benefits to being a good storyteller, but in many situations, it's good to try to shorten your story. Get to the point, so that you will be heard.

When I was coaching kids' sports teams, I used to bring along Q-tips. When the kids weren't doing a very good job of listening, I would hand them a Q-tip to make a point about opening up their ears.

In Principle #10, I will talk about respecting authority. One way to do that is to listen.

There was a time in my life when I always wanted to have the best story. If someone told me a good story about themselves, I would come back with one better. You know how it goes: Someone tells you about catching a two-pound fish, and you quickly respond with a story about your three-pound fish. Somebody says they had a tough time running a five-minute mile, and you can't wait to tell how you almost *died* running a five-minute mile because of how out of shape that you were.

I came to realize that this wasn't very nice. Telling your story can add to the conversation, but if it is just a way of topping your friend, then that's not being very friendly. We all need that good friend who just seems to understand us and care for us, but better yet is when you can be that person for someone else.

I recently had a discussion with one of my coworkers about how I use social media. I am connected to over a thousand people on a variety of social platforms. There's no way I could pay attention to that many people without the power of social media to stay in touch.

For example, this coworker began to talk about his daughter going to college. I could add a lot of value to the conversation, because I paid attention to his posts about visiting colleges with his daughter.

There's a guy in another city who has become a very good Facebook friend. We often comment on each other's posts. I feel like I know him pretty well and that we're pretty similar people, but at this point, we have never actually met in person.

One of the extreme cases of this was when a friend posted about his nephew being in intensive care in St. Louis. My family and I went out to eat one night, and I ran into this friend leaving the restaurant. Typically, we would have had a pretty generic, "Hi, how are you" conversation, but because I had read his posts, we could have a deep talk about the pain of his nephew's situation.

If I know that I am going to see someone, I will take the time to look at their social media, or if I see someone in a restaurant, I will pull up their Facebook page before going over to talk with them. It's amazing how much you can improve the quality of the conversation if you have some good information about what is going on in their life.

I am a huge fan of Chick-fil-A and love their Christian

principles and their leader, Dan Cathy. They proposed to give out free ice cream, if people would stay off their phones while they eat and talk with the people at their tables. While I agree with the concept, some of our best family times have happened while we're all sitting around a table looking at our phones. The difference is that we interact with each other about what we are seeing on our phones. It leads to good conversation.

As printed in *Wooden*, one of the "Seven Things to Do" John Wooden learned from his father was, "Make friendship a fine art." I define it as being intentional about being someone's friend.

One of my favorite things to do is to play "friend-liaison." Say I meet Fred, and he reminds me of Bob. I will then try to get Fred and Bob together, because I think their similarities will lead to a good friendship.

I recently met up with Dr. Rob Rienow at one of Kurtis' Olivet baseball games. Rob's son R. W. is on Kurtis' team. I watched Rob interacting with his kids at the game, and I knew there was something special about him. I introduced myself, and we had a simple conversation. I was able to discover that he and his wife have seven kids.

I went home and Googled Rob. I found out that he is a pastor who has developed a ministry called Visionary Family Ministries. Rob serves part time at a church in Wheaton, Ilinois, and also preaches once a month at a church in Minnesota. His sermons are online, and when I checked them out, I discovered that he has authored several books. As time has gone along, I have followed his posts on Facebook and listened to his sermons. I have then emailed him material that I've read, based upon what he was discussing. By being intentional about communicating with Rob, I feel like we have become friends. At the point of writing this, we have only met twice, but because I reached out, I feel like we have a relationship.

The Golden Rule says to treat others the way you would like to be treated. Emily mentioned in the intro to this book that the two big things in life are to love God and love your neighbor. Making friendship a fine art ties into these two. We must make an effort to be friends with God. He wants a relationship with us. He wants us to take time to be with him. On the other end, we need to put emphasis on loving our neighbor. What can I do to help that person grow?

One of the things that I am trying to accomplish with this book is to give you simple tools to not only help you raise your kids, but also to grow yourself and others. I find that these things really help me in being a good friend, as well.

My life verse these days is Luke 23:43 (ESV), where Jesus tells the repentant sinner on the cross, "Today you will be with me in Paradise." When someone posts about a death on Facebook, and I know that the person who passed away is a Christian, I can use this verse. I'll reply, "I'm so sorry for your loss, but take comfort that your loved one is in Paradise."

"There is Heaven. There is hell. There is Earth, with a little bit of both. Don't lose your Heaven while you are going through hell." There isn't a week that goes by that I don't post this or say this to somebody. I think it is comforting to people to acknowledge that they are hurting, but I also think this simple statement gives people hope that this is part of God's plan.

God has gotten me through a number of mistakes in my life, which often helps me in relating to people. Recently, I was talking with a guy who was going through a divorce. He was not happy with his soon-to-be ex-spouse to say the least. He acted as if there was no hope of staying in his daughter's life, so he might as well not bother trying. I have tried to be a good friend by encouraging him with the Heaven/hell statement. Thanks to modern technology, I can take one minute a couple days a week and text him something encouraging. I love to find images on Google that quote Bible verses or sayings.

It helps that I have been through a divorce. I can tell him my story. I recently sent him a picture of my grandson Eli's dedication, which includes my family and my ex-wife's family. I used this picture to make the point to him that he needed to stay in his daughter's life. I told him, "She needs her dad. To do that, you are going to have to find a way to forgive her mom. You are going to have to find a way to work with her mom. It's not easy, but it's necessary."

Life might be easier for us if we stay out of other people's business, but I believe that God called us to make friendship a fine art. Sometimes, that can get a little messy, but one day, God will give us our reward.

One of the best things I did with Kurtis was to introduce him to this saying: "Good, better, best, never let it rest, 'til your good is better, and your better is best." This proverb is often attributed to theologian Saint Jerome. According to Jeff Savage, Tim Duncan learned it as a nursery rhyme. Where I heard it was on a CD from Indianapolis Colts Chaplain Ken Johnson, who spoke at a Fellowship of Christian Athletes banquet.

Ken tells the story that as he was trying to work his way out of the ghetto, he had a teacher who was pretty hard on him. Ken was not very fond of hearing these words that she often used: "Good, better, best, never let it rest, 'til your good is better, and your better is best." Ken was happy making Ds on his report card. In his mind, he wasn't failing; that was his definition of success in the classroom. He was really impressed with himself when he improved to C work. Still, his teacher wanted more, and she was very demanding, until he finally got to the point of doing work that could honestly be graded as an A.

Ken Johnson's story is a pretty amazing one, in that he finally worked hard enough to get a football scholarship to Tulsa. Football came pretty naturally to him; it was the school work that was hard. How did his mom react to the scholarship? She shot him! Years of drugs and prostitution had warped her mind, and she was scared of her son leaving the ghetto. She had been taught that the white man was evil, and here her son was being dragged off to play football for the white guy. Fortunately for Ken, she used an old gun with a rusty bullet, which didn't penetrate very far into his arm.

It was great when I could text to Kurtis, "good, better, best," and he would then respond, "never let it rest, til your good is better and your better is best."

John Groce, when he was the head coach of the Illini basketball team, talked about the "1% solution." He wanted his guys to get 1% better each day. Kurtis' high school basketball coach, Tom Noonan, adopted this approach as well. He told his team, "If each day we can get a little bit better, down the road it's amazing where we will go."

Each year, your kids should be better than they were the year before. You need to figure out ways to measure their success. Some parents like to chart on the wall how a kid is growing taller; it is also important that you chart how a kid is growing in other ways. How are they improving in the classroom? Is it getting easier for them to get their chores done around the house? Are there activities that you no longer have to tell them to do? For example, people are coming over, and Mom says she wants things picked up. After doing this a few times, you shouldn't have to tell them specifically what to do any more.

I mentioned this on a few occasions that the goal is not to raise good kids; the goal is to raise good adults. Adults should get to the point where they don't need their parents for the everyday tasks of life. We all love to spoil our kids, but it should be an act of love, not a necessity for their survival.

1 Corinthians 15:33 NIV says, "Do not be misled: 'Bad company corrupts good character.'"

One of the most important habits your kids need to develop is to surround themselves with good people. Kurtis was so blessed to be surrounded by good, quality people and coaches. Dan Boyton did a tremendous job pouring into Kurtis' life. Dan led a program called Kairos where the kids went away for the week. As part of this, Suzanne and I wrote letters to Kurtis before he went, that he could read while there. In the letters, we took the time to tell him how special he was to us. Likewise, he wrote letters back saying how thankful he was for us as parents. Kairos was an extra special time, but Mister Boyton was always there for the kids during their everyday lives, as well.

Coach Noonan was a big influence, as well. He was a younger guy, so he related well to the kids. Coach Noonan had good parents who did a good job of setting his moral compass, which allowed him to pass that along to the kids he was leading. He was maybe a little bit too competitive on the basketball court, but the kids learned a great deal about teamwork and what was needed to be successful.

Kurt was so blessed to have a good friend in Adam Peters. We had a really tough decision to make when Kurt got to high school. Up to eighth grade, he had attended the Lutheran school in town and had a lot of good friends. However, the Catholic high school, Saint Teresa, had a better baseball program at the time and the prospects for really good teams during Kurt's four years. In addition, there was the possibility of developing a friendship with Adam, who was one of the area's better baseball players. Adam played with us a bit on the Champaign Tribe, and I knew Adam's family and knew that he came from good people. Things turned out as well as expected and even better. Adam was a first-class kid, and he and Kurtis could work hard together to do well in the classroom and on the athletic field.

In the intro, Emily talked about her good friends at the Lutheran school. Among her college friends, Dad would prefer that they had a little more Christian guidance, but they seem to be nice people with whom she has surrounded herself.

Peer pressure is a big deal. Marc Mero is a retired professional wrestler and motivational speaker, who does an amazing job of speaking to kids. As you can see in a YouTube video posted by Richie B, one of his sayings is, "You show me your friends; I will show you your future."

"How do I know that," he asks on the video. "I hung out with losers, and I became the biggest loser of them all." He goes on to talk about how he took his mom for granted. She was "the only one that ever believed in [him]," and he treated her poorly. Marc has brought many kids to tears, as he talks of his mother's death. Be sure to look up his speech on YouTube. You can learn more about Marc at ThinkPoz.org.

If you get in the wrong crowd, odds are you will get into trouble with them.

I first became familiar with Kenneth Blanchard, Ph.D., through a book, *The One Minute Manager*. It was one of the original business books I read back in the early 90's. It's designed as a business leadership book, but I think it also gives good leadership ideas for those who are leading kids. Of the three big parts of that book, the first is setting goals. How about doing that with your kids? It's important to let them know what you expect. We were very demanding with our kids; a grade of C was only appropriate for the neighbor's children, as I liked to say (another "Woodenism"). Our kids knew that we expected a lot, and we were fortunate that they delivered.

Blanchard's book goes on to talk about how important it is to praise. Tell your kids specifically what they did right. I have this weird thing inside of me that makes it hard for me to tolerate misbehavior. Of course, this is mostly in judging the behaviors of others, not in judging my own, but this little bug inside of me often caused me to let my kids know when I wasn't happy. Thankfully, the kids seemed to benefit from that as well.

I used to tell my kids to be smart or to make sure that they made good decisions, but as they became such good people, I changed that to, "Stay smart." Now that Kurtis is twenty-one and going out to places where people are drinking, I will say, "Stay smart, buddy," trying to keep him from making that one poor decision that can have huge consequences.

My pastor, Eric Trickey, gave our church the awesome

concept of "Pray3:16," based on John 3:16. A good habit is to always take things to the Lord in prayer. Each day, we should stop at 3:16 p.m. and pray to God for some wisdom to help us through the rest of the day. Of all the Bible verses, John 3:16 is one of the best to summarize the Christian faith. We are separated from God by our sinful nature. However, 3:16 tells us that God loved us so much that He sent His Son not to condemn us in our sin, but to save us and provide us a path to eternal life with Him.

Max Lucado wrote a book titled *3:16: The Numbers of Hope.* He describes the verse as:

> A twenty-six word parade of hope: beginning with God, ending with life, and urging us to do the same. Brief enough to write on a napkin or memorize in a moment, yet solid enough to weather two thousand years of storms and questions. If you know nothing of the Bible, start here. If you know everything in the Bible, return here. . . . The heart of the human problem is the heart of the human. And God's treatment is prescribed in John 3:16.

> *"For God so loved the world that he gave his one and only Son, that whoever believes in him shall not perish but have eternal life."--John 3:16 NIV*

There are 86,400 seconds in every day. How many of those seconds do you spend with God? We should at least be able to stop at 3:16 and spend a little time with Him.

Have you heard the story of Tim Tebow wearing John 3:16 under his eyes during the Bowl Championship Series (BCS) College Football Championship game on January 8, 2009? This seemingly small gesture resulted in ninety million people searching Google for that Bible verse.

Three years later to the day, January 8, 2012, Tebow had one of his few successful games as an NFL quarterback, when he led the Denver Broncos to a playoff victory over the Pittsburg Steelers. Denver had lost their last three games, by an average of sixteen points. Pittsburg threw a touchdown pass to send the game into overtime, but on the first play of OT, Tebow was able to hook up with a wide receiver for an eighty-yard touchdown to win the game. What added to the amazement was that this completion had Tebow finish the game with 316 yards passing. He did that on just ten completed passes, so he averaged 31.6 yards per completion. He also averaged 3.16 yards every time he rushed the ball. The Pittsburgh quarterback threw a key interception on third down and sixteen. Pittsburgh had the ball for thirty-one minutes and six seconds. I'm not sure how many people saw the game, but the Nielsen rating for the game was 31.6. On Monday morning, what was the most Googled phrase? John 3:16. (You can watch Tim Tebow tell this story in a YouTube video posted by Above Inspiration.)

Maybe your Pray3:16 won't result in ninety million Google searches, but I know it will help you keep your day in focus. And you never know who might be watching.

I recently reconnected on Facebook with a guy I played baseball with in college. We hadn't spoken in thirty years. As we began to follow each other on Facebook, he saw some of my Pray3:16 posts. He shared with me that he was going through a rough patch and was struggling with his faith. I was able to share a few things with him, and he has embraced the Pray3:16 concept. He recently posted that only when we kneel before God can we stand before mankind.

My church recently completed a program called "Be the Message," which focused on the fact that Christianity must be lived out. One way to share hope is by posting Pray3:16 on your Facebook page or letting people know that you are praying for them. Maybe you can come up with a list of 316 things to pray for, or maybe you just want to pray for 31.6 seconds. Whatever you choose to do, this time of connection with God will be a source of strength and focus for your day.

In 2017, Pastor Eric shared this concept at a Chamber of Commerce prayer breakfast. He started with Acts 3:19 NIV: "Repent, then, and turn to God, so that your sins may be wiped out, that times of refreshing may come from the Lord,[.]" It seemed like quite the God thing when, without any prior discussion, keynote speaker Sonya Jones followed that up with 2 Chronicles 7:14 and a pray at 7:14 concept. She joked that with her version you could sleep in four more hours. Sonya was on Season 16 of the TV show, *The Biggest Loser*. She started at 283 pounds and worked her way down to 144 by the end of the show. She shared about how the show was not only about her physical health, but her psychological health as well. She had learned how to love herself again and battle her binge eating.

She also focused on this word: repent. When we look at 2 Chronicles 7:14 in the New International Version, it says, "if my people, who are called by my name, will humble themselves and pray and seek my face and turn from their wicked ways, then I will hear from heaven, and I will forgive their sin and will heal their land."

So what does a good rhythm look like for your kids? Getting plenty of sleep, eating a balanced diet, eating what is fixed for them, responding on the first or second call, listening well, completing homework without too much procrastination or objection, getting some physical exercise, making good friends, doing something every day to get better and having a devotional and prayer life including church on the weekends.

I have often described it that for me, going to church is like taking out the garbage. It just seems to get rid of all the bad from the previous week, and it gives me a fresh start on the coming week. When I am whining, complaining and making excuses, church seems to get me back in the proper state of mind. It is the best habit of all.

*James W. Minton, Sr. (Jim)*

James 5:19-20 NIV: "My brothers and sisters, if one of you should wander from the truth and someone should bring that person back, remember this: Whoever turns a sinner from the error of their way will save them from death and cover over a multitude of sins."

# Enjoy Word entertainment.

One of the smartest things we did was to raise our kids on Christian music. In the first chapter, we talked about the difference the "L" can make, going from world to Word. It is the same with your music.

We started our kids off with Geoff Moore and the Distance and their song called "Home Run." It was a song that blended baseball with Jesus.

The band has another song called "Why Should the Devil (Have All the Good Music)." This is a line they attributed to Martin Luther, explaining that he took the hymns of the day and put them to the music of German bar songs.

But one of their songs that really hit home with me was "New Americans":

> Never has there been a group more patriotic-less
> As the bells of freedom ring in the name of liberty
> We run down each other chasing the American dream
> Who will help to lead the way back to what made our land so great?
> Is there anyone who will say,
> "This is God's country?"

*James W. Minton, Sr. (Jim)*

This song was so powerful that I ended up doing a presentation on it at a Fellowship of Christian Athletes meeting.

I have heard a phrase used in business about being able to work while you sleep. For example, if you can put together a good website, it can be telling your story for you while you are occupied with other things. If you can develop a good referral network, you benefit from word of mouth marketing. That is how I look at getting your kids involved in Christian music. It can help tell the story of Jesus' love, so you don't have to beat your kids over the head with the message.

We are fortunate in Decatur to have the annual Decatur Celebration festival. Each summer, a couple of Christian groups perform during this event. For many years, my family went on a mini-vacation to my company's annual conference just before the Celebration. I would purchase the CDs from the Christian groups who were going to perform, and as we travelled, we learned the lyrics. Then we could sing along with the bands when we saw them live. It was great fun, but it was also a great lesson.

One year, it was Avalon and their hit, "Testify to Love": "For as long as I shall live, I will testify to love. I'll be a witness in the silences when words are not enough... with every breath I take, I will give thanks to God above, and as long as I shall live, I will testify to love."

At the time he appeared, Mark Schultz had a popular song, "He's My Son," in which he is praying for a boy who is really sick. I would also love to print all the words to Mark's song "I Am the Way." I encourage you to look up that song and give it a listen.

However, my favorite Mark Schultz song is "Let's Go": "You got a nice job and an office on the second floor. But you are looking out the window and you are thinking there is something more. You clear your head. You close your eyes and something deep inside you cries, 'Let's go!'" Great words to inspire us to be involved in the mission field!

It is such a blessing to hear your children singing along to

78

the words of a Christian song, proclaiming that Jesus is the way. Now I get to hear my four-year-old grandson doing it, as well.

When I was first trying to act a little stronger in my Christian faith, I remember going into a bookstore in Springfield and purchasing a yellow-colored CD of Christian greatest hits. One of the songs on that CD was "Jesus Freak" by DC Talk. When Kurtis started playing and traveling with the Champaign Tribe baseball team, we boomed this song out of our stereo system as we drove. Half the time, Kurtis would fall asleep on the way, but evidently the lyrics still got through. Now when Kurtis identifies himself on the Twitter feed, he calls himself a "Jesus freak."

The chorus of the DC Talk song is:

What will people think
When they hear that I'm a Jesus freak?
What will people do
When they find that's it's true?

Toby McKeehan, who calls himself TobyMac, was one of the members of DC Talk when they performed this song. In my eyes, TobyMac is on the same level as John Wooden, and that is saying something! I'm amazed that Toby is a month older than I am, yet he is still out there performing with a tremendous amount of energy.

One of my great joys is taking my family to Christian music shows, and some of the best times of my life have been at TobyMac concerts. The absolute top experience was when it was arranged for us to go backstage at the Illinois State Fair to meet Toby in person. I was able to tell him that we named our dog after him. Toby's longtime sidekick, Gabrielle, got a good chuckle out of that, but Toby responded that he thought it was an honor.

Music will always be a major form of expression. I think most of us like the style of music that was popular when we were in high school. My dad loves the Big Band sound, because that is what he grew up with. Many people are big fans of songs from the 1950s. My generation grew up with a lot of great rock bands, with a side dose of Willie Nelson and Lynyrd Skynyrd. Today's hip hop music seems especially hard on our kids. While lots of music inspires us to poor behavior, hip hop seems especially bad. Christian music inspires us to proper behavior.

One time, Emily had a friend over, and TobyMac's "Lose my Soul" came on the radio. "This is my dad's theme song," Emily told her friend. After the intro, the song begins:

> Father God, I am clay in Your Hands,
> Help me to stay that way
> through all life's demands,
> 'Cause they chip, and they nag,
> and they pull at me,
> And every little thing I make up my mind to be,
> . . .
> Though it's only in You that I can truly see
> That it's a feast for the eyes, a low blow to purpose,
> And I'm a little kid at a three ring circus.
> I don't want to gain the whole world
> and lose my soul.

I thought about contrasting these "Word" songs I've mentioned with some of the lyrics that are available in "world" music, but I don't even know where to start. I'm sure you can think of some examples of stuff that isn't exactly appropriate for your kids to listen to. Much of it is probably not that bad; I suppose that Jimmy Buffet's "Margaritaville" isn't going to cause our kids to become drunken layabouts. However, a constant barrage of worldly values does weigh on them, and when I'm at the gas station and see kids in car seats hearing songs with inappropriate four-letter words that talk about the benefits of the gangster life, I don't think that is going to end well.

Today we are blessed to have all different forms of Christian music. If you like the hip hop sound, there are rappers like Lecrae and Andy Mineo. Jamie Grace might give an alternative to other female singers. Skillet has become one of my favorite hard rock bands; its members include Korey and John Cooper, Seth Morrison and Jen Ledger.

I love the story of Jen Ledger, the female drummer for Skillet. It's fun to listen to her tell her testimony in a YouTube video posted by Obsessive Hope because Jen has a British accent. She talks about growing up in the Church of England but not having a personal relationship with Christ. When she was sixteen, she had a chance to go to a Bible camp in Kenosha, Wisconsin. Just before she made her trip across the sea, she really discovered in her heart who Jesus is.

As Piet Levy reports on the *Post-Crescent* website, Kenosha, Wisconsin's Living Light Christian Church was co-founded by Korey Cooper's parents, Timothy and Carol Pingatore. After they were married, Korey and John Cooper moved to Kenosha. (Historically, Skillet has shared their lyrics with the pastor of Living Light Christian Church before performing them in front of the public to be sure the lyrics were "theologically sound.")

The Virtuous Girls website reports that, when Skillet was looking for a drummer, Jen Ledger was a good friend of Rosalie Pingatore, Korey Cooper's sister, and it was through that connection that Jen became part of the band and is now able to share her passion for Jesus through music.

Skillet has done some amazing things in the Christian music world, selling millions and millions of records. I believe there will be some people in Heaven that wouldn't have been there without the music Skillet plays. It amazes me how God connected a girl from England with a band from Wisconsin, but I am sure glad He did, as I love their music and ministry.

I would love to tell you that my kids didn't watch any junk on TV, but it didn't turn out that way. Emily was always a big fan of the show *Teen Mom*. She also enjoys some of the shows with vapid humor. She and Kurtis were big fans of *Spongebob Squarepants*, which I will never understand.

We are fortunate that Phil Vischer started *Veggie Tales*. What an interesting concept, helping kids learn the Bible through a bunch of talking vegetables!

It was always fun to have a movie night with the family. There used to be lots of shows with good, wholesome family values, but now there have to be specific movies made for the Christian community.

One of the first to come out was *Facing the Giants*. In this film, Coach Grant Taylor is having a rough go of it. Everything is struggling, including his football team, so he decides to take a new approach and begins praising God, no matter what.

One of the great scenes in the movie is when one of Taylor's players does what they called a "death crawl," traveling the entire length of a football field on all fours, while blindfolded and carrying another player on his back. The coach is making the point that we can accomplish incredible things if we don't limit ourselves.

The acting in the movie was pretty suspect. The story was a bit predictable. However, the Christian message clearly comes through.

*Courageous* is a movie that revolves around being a good father. The lead character Mitchell's daughter is killed by a drunk driver. As he struggles with her death, he begins to study what the Bible has to say about fatherhood. He realizes he needs to do a better job of loving his son and composes a multi-point resolution to honor God in each and every aspect of his family life. The movie was not only entertaining, but it also presented a great message to the kids about family.

When your child is old enough, *The Passion of the Christ* is a must-watch. It really makes the point of how much Jesus had to suffer for our sins.

I love the story of Michael Lorenzen of the Cincinnati Reds. As he tells his story in a YouTube video posted by Renewed Strength Fitness, he grew up in a dysfunctional home, with an alcoholic father who ended up deserting the family. Michael was always a very talented baseball player, but he had trouble staying out of trouble. He tells the story of being on a California pier, high after smoking marijuana, when a man begins to share the gospel with him.

Does it really work to share the gospel with somebody who's high? Well, in Michael's case, it did. One of the reasons it worked is because he and his friends had recently gone to see *The Passion of the Christ*. The movie did a good job of setting up what the man on the beach was trying to share.

I first became aware of Michael's story when I saw that he had a "116" tattoo to associate himself with a group of Christian rappers called the 116 Clique. As Patricia Hoskins mentions in her article about the group, they revolve their mission around Romans 1:16 (NIV): "For I am not ashamed of the gospel [of Jesus Christ]."

Through my work as a retirement planner, I ran into a movie titled *The Ultimate Gift*, based on the book of the same name. It was the last feature-length film that James Garner appeared in before his death in 2014, and in which he played the role of a rich Texas oil man who is dying. Before his death, the man makes a series of recordings to help his grandson, Jason Stevens, who currently is a spoiled brat. Jason's dad was killed in an airplane accident, and people felt sorry for Jason. Through their misguided sympathy, they ended up turning him into a rotten young man who thought money grew on trees, and it was his right to spend it all.

In order to receive the inheritance from his grandfather, Jason has to learn twelve lessons, including the value of hard work, how to be a friend and what it is like to lose it all. He ends up finding true love and getting the millions. Not to spoil the movie for you, but in the final scene, Jason gives a great deal of the money away.

Media is powerful. That can be a good thing or a bad thing.

Actor Sean Astin, well-known for his role in *Rudy*, got involved in making Christian movies and helped raise the quality. Sean had the lead role in *Woodlawn*, an awesome movie about racial tension in the South and how God worked through the Fellowship of Christian Athletes to provide a solution.

It was an awesome experience to go to the movie theater and see *God's Not Dead*. At the end of the movie, it instructs you to text your friends: "God is NOT dead." It was so great to see my kids participate in that.

In Christian rapper Lecrae Moore's book, *Unashamed*, and in a YouTube video posted by Bossip, he talks about the nature of hip hop music. He believes it celebrates the culture that he grew up in. However, I feel that worldly hip hop music also celebrates a sin culture. If you raise your kids on music that celebrates sin, don't be shocked when they end up living it out. Likewise, when you raise your kids on Christian music and movies, don't be shocked when they end up living it out.

## Is the internet good or bad?

The answer is . . . yes!

I am sure many of you have sat down on a Saturday morning for a quick glance at Facebook, only to find your day completely getting away from you. I know how much you love those political posts from that friend (maybe even me) who has a different opinion or challenges your thoughts. I won't even get into the fact that there are millions of pages on the internet devoted to pornography. The point is, never before has it been so easy to get into some bad habits.

However, there is also an incredible amount of good information that is available to us. I am not much of a handyman, but when I can Google something and watch a video on how to do it, it improves my chances of success. Plus, how about that great recipe you found on Pinterest?

Kids today are attached to their phones, so we can either fight them on it or roll with it. In the introduction, I mentioned that Kurtis and Emily turned out pretty good. One of the things that I think was part of their success was the fact that I embraced the internet. Instead of just lecturing them, I had a tool that I could use to show them right and wrong. The wrong seemed to have a way of finding them; it was up to me to show them the way to the right.

It is always great to have some family devotional time. What I often did for ours was to have a "video of the week." If I came across a particular Christian video that really jumped out at me, I would sit down with Suzanne and the kids to watch and discuss it together.

Baseball player Albert Pujols was a St. Louis Cardinal and always at the top of the list for good, Christian interviews to watch. Fellow Cardinals Matt Holiday and Adam Wainwright were not far behind. I also loved to share videos of Chicago Cub Ben Zobrist.

One way to figure out who the Christian baseball players are is to listen when someone comes up to bat. Players pick out a favorite song to be played as they walk up to the plate. For Zobrist in his World Series year with the Cubs, it was his wife Julianna's song, "Alive." I love to listen to this song. It is even better when you know the story about how Julianna came to write it.

She shares in a YouTube video she posted that Ben came home from baseball one night and told her about a fellow ballplayer, "a rough dude, just kind of rough around the edges in every way," who came to the conclusion that, "I think I got saved." Ben said that as his teammate talked about his new faith, about how "the Lord was working in his life," the man stated that for the first time in his life he felt truly alive.

Ben Zobrist also made several videos for Olivet Nazarene University, available on YouTube, in which he does an incredible job of sharing his faith.

The stories on ESPN's show *E:60* are often interesting. There was a great episode about Ed Thomas, a football coach in Iowa, whose family was awarded the 2010 Arthur Ashe Courage Award. One of Ed's former football players was having some mental struggles, and he ended up fatally shooting the coach. The episode tells how Ed's family embraced the shooter's family; it is a great story of forgiveness and showing Christian character.

The Skit Guys also put out some powerful material, with their video "God's Chisel" being at the top of my list.

IAmSecond.com is an awesome website to check out. The name comes from the premise that we should put God and others ahead of ourselves. The website provides a series of videos in which famous people are interviewed about their faith. The presentation makes quite an impression, as the people sit in a white chair with just one light overhead, and the background is nothing but black. Lecrea has a really good interview. I also loved the video of Los Angeles Dodgers pitcher Clayton Kershaw. Arguably the best pitcher in baseball, he has a humble heart for the Lord.

There is a show out of Canada called *Full Circle* (a spinoff of *100 Huntley Street*), which is kind of a Christian version of *The View*. If you look up the show's website (100Huntley.com) or YouTube channel (100huntley) online, you can find lots of good interviews they have done. I found a really interesting one on YouTube they did with a woman named Pattie Mallette.

Pattie tells her story about how she was a complete mess. As she tried to find Jesus, she kept falling back into a life of sin. Finally, she ended up in a hospital after attempting suicide. A local pastor brought her a beautiful flower and told her, "This is how God sees you." After that experience, Pattie was able to turn her life around and become a successful single parent. The interview then turns to the singing success of Pattie's young son, who got his start singing in the church. They finish by bringing the young man out for his first appearance on television. You might have heard of him: His name is Justin Bieber!

Whenever there were articles about kids getting in trouble or dying in drunk driving accidents, I always made sure to show my children the story. I would discuss with them how the choices they made could have very serious consequences.

When my kids went off to college, it was a little less stressful for me than it could have been because I had developed the habit of having a running text conversation with them. The kids were always busy going here and there and hanging out with friends, but they always had their phones with them. I could shoot them a text, and they would usually reply. As a result, it wasn't as big a deal for me when they went off to college because I could still communicate with them regularly through texting.

Social media is a really big deal to kids today. It's important that you know what is showing up on your kids' phones. I never tried to control the bad stuff. I just hoped that by providing enough good influences, my kids would be smart enough to stay away the bad stuff on their own. I think it has worked.

# Don't be a victim.

*You can make mistakes, but you aren't a failure until you start blaming others for those mistakes.*--*John Wooden* (from *Wooden*)

*"Neither this man nor his parents sinned," said Jesus, "but this happened so that the works of God might be displayed in him."*-- *John 9:3 NIV*

One of the worst things you can do in life is live as a victim. I am always amazed by stories of people who are faced with extremely tough situations, such as a disabling injury or sickness, yet they persevere to live life as normally as possible and find a way to keep a smile on their faces. John Wooden, the famous basketball coach, commented that you are not a loser until you blame someone else.

Have you ever bought any of those "as seen on TV" products? There is a reason that they are being advertised at midnight as a $19.95 special. I just knew my wife was going to love her Pocket Hose, "The hose that grows," when I presented it to her on Mother's Day. She hated having to carry around the heavy hose. This was going to be perfect to have such a light hose for when she got up on the roof to clean the gutters. (What? I have bad knees!) To say the least, things did not work out as expected. It was pretty quickly determined that the hose was useless.

Likewise, I think we have to be careful when someone tells

us we are a victim. You appreciate that they have acknowledged your tough spot in life, but it may be that their empathy is of little value. An example of this is politicians. They are constantly telling us we are victims. When oil prices were high, we were the victim of those greedy oil companies. We were told everything would be better once we were no longer victims of President Bush. Now, we are the victims of those terrible insurance companies; if we can just get rid of them, everything will be OK. We are all faced with tough obstacles in life. If you are counting on government to be the solution to your problems, you probably always will be a victim.

I think former Secretary of State Condaleeza Rice (quoted by Robert Gehrke) said it well: "America has never had a narrative of grievance. We've never believed, 'I am doing poorly because you're doing well.' The moment we begin to believe that we are doing badly because someone else is doing well, that moment that aggrievement takes over, it's not long before his twin brother comes behind, and that would be entitlement."

In Principle #10, we are going to talk about respecting authority, which includes umpires. Could you imagine a pregame speech that went something like this:

You guys have practiced hard to get ready for this big game. But now that I see who the refs are, you might as well give up. There is really no reason to play your hardest because you just know that the referees are going to take the game away from you. Instead of focusing on what you can do to win the game, be sure and keep track of every call that goes against you. Don't worry when we lose because we will have a good excuse. We can say that we were a victim of the referees.

The best example of perseverance that I know of is Nick Vujicik. Nick was born with no arms and no legs. I am very jealous of Nick. I would like people to buy my book and listen to my message, too, but I have all my limbs and a pretty effortless lifestyle. It's much easier to capture people's attention if you are blessed to overcome an amazing struggle. Of course, I am only kidding, but in order for a miracle to occur, you first have to have a very difficult set of circumstances. While I was coaching the kids' teams, if the team fell behind by a large margin, I would joke that the first thing you have to do to have a miraculous victory is get down by a bunch of runs, so we had accomplished the first stage in our plan. My goal with this approach was to get the kids to quit thinking about their predicament and get them thinking about the possibilities.

Too often when we come up against difficult circumstances, we give in. We quit fighting. We think, "Poor me, the victim!"

Nick Vujicic was born in Australia in 1982, the son of Yugoslavian immigrants. He was born with tetra-amelia, a condition where your limbs are not formed. In *Life Without Limits*, Nick recounts how his mother initially refused to hold him or even look at him. However, Nick's parents eventually accepted his condition and understood it as God's plan for their son.

According to the (*Daily*) *Mail* Foreign Service, "Nick has a small foot on his left hip," which he calls his "chicken drumstick." Nick adds, "I'd be lost without it." He uses his foot to write, type, pick things up, operate his electric wheelchair, surf, skateboard, and even play soccer. Although he did attempt suicide at age ten, "with the help of his religion, friends and family, Nick managed to pull through and become an international symbol of triumph over adversity." Knowing full well the bullying he would doubtlessly encounter, Nick's parents decided not to enroll him in a school for children with special needs and insisted he attend the mainstream schools. Now Nick is grateful for this decision. "It was the best decision they could have made for me. It was very hard but it gave me independence."

In an article about Nick, Jennifer Riley notes that at age seventeen, "Vujicic began giving inspirational speeches at school and church-sponsored events." She notes that "his message is especially understood by teenagers, who often feel lonely, rejected, confused and broken." Nick explains, "When I get up onstage, they know that I've been broken."

The Mail Foreign Service notes that Nick holds a degree in financial planning and real estate, and Riley notes, "Through his ministry, Life Without Limits, Vujicic travels around the world to share his inspiring personal testimony about how he found joy and hope in Jesus Christ despite his difficult and painful circumstances."

Riley quotes Nick explaining where he is in life and in faith: "That's where I am. That's the freedom and victory I have. I believe in a God who can do all things, but if He chooses not to give me arms and legs, I know it's for the better. And I may not understand it, but all I need to know is that He's going to carry me through--that there is a purpose for it."

If anyone had the chance to whine, complain and make excuses, it would be Nick, yet he took an incredibly difficult situation and turned it into an inspiration for people around the world.

Nick detailed his life and faith in his book, *Life Without Limits*. My son J. J. gave the book to me, but I set it aside, as I was busy doing some presentations on John Wooden. When I had time to review the book, I discovered what a perfect example it is of not being a victim of your circumstances. It also fit well with one of Wooden's lessons I had just spoken on. In *Coach Wooden One-On-One*, he talks about focusing on what you can control: "The more concerned we become over the things we can't control, the less we will do with the things we can control."

Why do bad things happen to good people? Nick's situation reminds me of the ninth chapter of the Gospel of John, which tells the story of Jesus healing a blind man. The disciples ask whose sin caused the man to be blind. Jesus replies that he was born blind so that Jesus could be glorified.

Nick has a lot of great material, but I think one of his best presentations happened when he appeared on Oprah Winfrey's TV show, *Oprah's Lifeclass*. Oprah told the audience that her co-host, noted pastor Rick Warren, had stated that Nick was "one of the best examples of winning the hand you're dealt." Oprah followed that up with, "This is gonna shut your mouth!"

During his presentation, Nick began, "God didn't give me this pain, but what the enemy tried to use for bad, He turned into good." Then he jumped up a step on a flight of stairs, a step that appeared to be almost a third of Nick's own height. He continued, "We are wonderfully and fearfully made from God."

I'll finish this story later, but right now I want to give you some other things to ponder.

It is interesting how sometimes when God takes something away, He gives something so much more. I remember when Patrick Henry Hughes spoke at the Decatur Illinois Community Leaders Breakfast. Patrick was born without eyes and was unable to fully straighten his arms and legs, leaving him confined to a wheelchair. Despite Patrick's disabilities, his dad introduced him to the piano when he was only nine months old.

Patrick's national fame began in 2006, while he was a student at the University of Louisville. At the suggestion of Louisville's marching band director, Dr. Greg Byrne, Patrick joined the Louisville Marching Band, playing trumpet while his father pushed him in his wheelchair through the marching routines. This visible commitment attracted increasing crowd and media attention throughout the fall football season, and the pair received a wide variety of television and newspaper coverage. Patrick was subsequently invited to play piano and sing in musical performances throughout the country, including two performances at the Grand Ole Opry.

Another great example of, "Don't be a victim!"

As shown in a YouTube video posted by salemleader, part of Patrick's message revolves around the first three letters of his name, P.A.T.:

The P is for passion, patience and perseverance. 'Cause in order to achieve a goal, you've got to have a passion for that goal. Be patient! It might take a while for your goal to work. You have to persevere. Keep trying! Don't give up!

The A is ability and attitude. Use the abilities that you know you have. Plus, keep a positive attitude.

And finally, the T is trust. Trust in yourself. You will achieve your goal eventually.

Following this explanation, Patrick Henry Hughes performs a moving rendition of the Brooks and Dunn song, "I Believe."

Patrick's dad refused to let him have a victim mentality.

We have to understand that God is God, and He has a plan. A little quote that I keep on my desk says, "God is bigger than your past, your depression, your pain, your hate, your anger, your doubt, your fear, your shame, your eating disorder, your self-harm, your anxiety, your loneliness, your scars, this world." Previously in this book, I talked about my struggles with a coach at St. Xavier University who made things difficult for me. I felt like I was a victim of an abusive coach, but in reality he was just trying to bring out the best in me.

In the biblical story of Joseph, the key theme is that his brothers meant him harm, but God used it for good. Joseph refused to be a victim.

Joseph's story is found in Genesis, chapters thirty-seven through fifty. He was the youngest of Jacob's eleven sons. As a young shepherd, Joseph brought a bad report about his brothers to their father. This behavior, plus the realization that Joseph was Jacob's favorite, caused his older brothers to have a great deal of animosity towards Joseph. When Jacob presented Joseph with a special coat of many colors, his brothers were about at the limit of what they could take. The final straw came when Joseph began relating his dreams about how he would rule over his family one day. The hatred towards Joseph peaked, and his brothers started plotting to kill him. However, Reuben, the eldest, objected to outright murder, so instead the brothers sold Joseph as a slave and deceived their father into thinking his favorite son had been slain by a wild animal.

Joseph was sold to a high-ranking Egyptian named Potiphar. This actually worked out well. In Genesis chapter thirty-nine, we read of how Joseph was very good at his job and turned out to be one of Potiphar's most trusted servants. Eventually, Joseph even became the supervisor of Potiphar's household. (It makes me think of the expression "turning lemons into lemonade," but I'm not sure that was done in biblical times.)

Potiphar could see that whatever Joseph did, God looked favorably on him. However, the devil never goes down without a fight. Potiphar's wife started to take a strong liking to Joseph, in an inappropriate way. Joseph resisted the temptation, which infuriated her, so she falsely accused him of attempted rape. Despite his innocence, Joseph was cast into prison. It looked like it was going to be a great story with a happy ending, but then Joseph found himself in jail.

"Don't be a victim" is about an attitude, a belief that God is not out to harm you, although He will put you through some tests. He is going to give you weights to lift and burdens to bear. The Grammy award-winning Christian singer Mandisa has an amazing song about being an "Overcomer." In the chorus, she sings:

> Stay in the fight 'til the final round
> You're not going under
> 'Cause God is holding you right now
> You might be down for a moment
> Feeling like it's hopeless
> That's when He reminds you
> That you're an overcomer

Be a victor, not a victim!

So again, Joseph didn't quit. While in jail, he interpreted the dreams of two of his fellow prisoners, which ended up coming true. One of the men was later released from jail and restored to his position as the king's cupbearer. Two years later, the king himself had some troubling dreams, and the cupbearer remembered Joseph's gift of interpretation. The king called for Joseph and related his dreams. Joseph predicted seven years of bountiful harvests, followed by seven years of severe famine in Egypt. He advised the king to begin storing grain in preparation for the coming struggles. For his wisdom, Joseph was made a ruler in Egypt, second only to the king.

Now it was time for Joseph and his brothers to meet again. Canaan was also affected by the drought, and Jacob sent ten of his sons to Egypt to buy grain. While there, they met their long-lost brother, whom they did not recognize. Joseph's brothers bowed down to him, fulfilling his earlier prophecy. Joseph then revealed his identity to his brothers and forgave their wrongdoing.

Joseph was a good winner (Principle #5).

There may be many circumstances where we are the victim of the situation. One time when Kurtis was going through a rough patch, I said, "I know things are bad, but don't make them any worse than they are." I think we often take something that is a six on the pain meter and make it into a nine. If you can have a "Don't be a victim" attitude, maybe you can dial that down to a four, instead of turning up the volume. It won't eliminate the pain, but a good attitude can make many things in life more bearable.

God can be complicated. Jeremiah 29:11 NIV proclaims, "'For I know the plans I have for you,' declares the LORD, 'plans to prosper you and not to harm you, plans to give you hope and a future.'" However, I also know that some of Jesus' disciples died horrible deaths. Many good, Christian parents have been though pain I can't even imagine, the grief of having to bury one of your kids.

Joseph's story presents insight into how God's sovereignty works to overcome evil and bring about His plan. In all his ordeals, Joseph was able to see God's hand at work. As he reveals his identity to his brothers in Genesis 45 NIV, Joseph speaks of their sin this way: "Do not be distressed and do not be angry with yourselves for selling me here, because it was to save lives that God sent me ahead of you. . . . It was not you who sent me here, but God." Joseph finishes in Genesis 50:20 NIV with, "You intended to harm me, but God intended it for good to accomplish what is now being done, the saving of many lives."

Before I finish up the story of Nick Vujicic, I would like to tell you the story of Michael Collins. I told you I can't imagine the grief of having to bury one of your kids. Jim Collins knows that agony; his son Michael was the victim of a drunk driver. Every parent's worst nightmare is to hear that late-night doorbell-ring of a policeman coming to tell you about an accident. Jim tells the story of this loss, and the amazing things that happened afterwards, in his book, *Uncommon Hope*.

Jim was one of our archrivals when I played fastpitch softball. Jim was a great hitter, with an unusual batting style that really made him stand out. We had some terrific battles when Jim was with the Bloomington Hearts, and I was playing for the Decatur Pride. I had caught back up with Jim when he was coaching the eighteen-and-under baseball team in Bloomington, and Kurtis was playing for the Decatur Commodores.

Michael was a good baseball player at Heartland Community College. One of his greatest moments was hitting a home run during the 2012 Junior College World Series. Jim didn't get to see Michael's home run because he was coaching the Normal University High School team to a state championship. After Michael finished his playing days, he started serving as an assistant coach for his dad's team.

Michael was a senior at Illinois State University when he lost his life. He was headed back to his apartment after a dance, when a woman slammed her vehicle into the car in which Michael was a passenger. The impact was directly into Michael's door, at a speed as high as 130 miles per hour.

In the book, Jim talks about how difficult it was for him when it was time to go back and coach his team after this tragedy. He had lost his son, but he also felt for the guys who had lost their assistant coach. Jim didn't think he had the strength to do it, until he made a trip to the cemetery to "talk" with Michael. The next day, Jim went for a walk around a golf course by their house where he and Michael had played many times. I would highly recommend that you check out the book to see how the details played out, but basically Jim was moved by the spirit of Michael to be there for his team.

The book goes on to tell stories about how Jim helped various players on the team get through this tragedy and, in the process, began to heal himself. Michael had signed up to be an organ donor, so it gave some comfort to the family that Michael's organs were going to help others live.

But then this "mess" really got turned into a "mess-age" when the Pay It Forward for Michael Collins campaign got rolling. It all started with one of Michael's friends, Hailey Lanier, who started promoting random acts of kindness. She and some friends created cards to hand out, which inspired people to start paying for those in line behind them at the drive-up, leaving extra large tips and genuinely thinking of others.

At the time, Kurtis was playing baseball at Saint Teresa High School. At a game against Okaw Valley, the "Saint T." parents pitched in and bought pizza for both teams to enjoy together after the game. As the kids got their food, they were each handed a card that said not to drink and drive and to find a way to "pay it forward" to honor Michael's memory.

We don't see public education doing much with God any more, but the Illinois High School Association website featured an article on the Pay It Forward campaign started by Hailey

Lanier. The story started off by discussing a Bible study that Michael had been part of that was based on Tony Dungy's book, *Dare to Be Uncommon*. As part of the Bible study, the kids were challenged to write their own obituaries. In bold print, the article presented the last two lines of what Michael wrote for himself: "**He was a strong believer in Jesus Christ and helped others look to follow God. He enjoyed making people laugh until he died.**"

Sometimes when people pass away suddenly, you wonder where they stood with Christ. Not this guy!

It was reported in the IHSA article that the Pay It Forward for Michael Collins campaign (#MCstrong), started in Bloomington-Normal, had spread to forty-three states and fifteen different countries in just one month.

I am sure Jim and his wife Kelly and Michael's many friends and relatives will tell you that you never really get over something like this. Michael's uncle, Jeff, often posts on Facebook about times when Michael's number, nineteen, shows up in unusual places; thoughts of Michael are continually with those who loved him. But rather than focus on the bitter pain of their loss, they have chosen to focus on making this world a better place, to honor his memory.

Bad things often happen to good people. The world can be brutally unfair, but the question is: Will that make you bitter, or will it make you better?

When you have a victim mentality, you always have a good excuse. You always have a reason to whine and complain. What was the second set of John Wooden's two sets of threes? Don't whine. Don't complain. Don't make excuses.

You will always have a reason to quit. That, in a nutshell, is the problem that comes with being a victim. Life is hard; it takes all the effort that we have. Any time that we lose focus or feel like the opponent is just too much, we slack off and don't give it our best effort.

In baseball, a person who fails 70% of the time is successful. I have joked with kids I've coached that you have to be pretty dumb to remain confident in your abilities, when you know that you are going to fail 70% of the time, but if you don't remain convinced that you are going to get a hit every time you go to the plate, you are never going to bat .300.

I think it is similar with life. Yes, you are going to get the short end of the stick, but as soon as you end up with a victim mentality, you are not going to be able to do the best with what you have been given.

Now, back to Nick Vujicik's appearance with Oprah. If you remember, despite not having any limbs, he had navigated up one step of a staircase.

Nick goes on to talk about loving Porsches over Ferraris, contrasting the value of expensive cars to the value of people. He says, "I want everyone to know that we are wonderfully and fearfully made, and until you can actually understand that we are all wonderfully and fearfully made from God, I want you to know that you will always be trapped and chained, and you will be stopped. But when you have the incredible power of faith in action, nothing holds you back, and you're beautiful just the way that you are."

Nick then jumps up to the second step. He continues with, "All things come together for the good for those who love Him."

Nick's second jump puts him high up on the staircase, and it is now becoming a pretty good fall if he were to tumble off the stairs. He jokes that he's getting high enough that he's afraid he might break an arm. He then says, "It's all about choice. . . . I had parents who were my heroes. They always said, 'You can either be angry for what you don't have or be thankful for what you do have. Do your best, and God will do the rest.'"

Nick now makes it up to the third stair; two more to go. He says, "Because I gave my life to the Lord Jesus Christ"--He hops up to the fourth stair--"and the renewing of my mind"--He quickly hops up the last step--"I knew that I could be unstoppable!"

He gets a roaring round of applause, as he proves beyond any doubt that he is not a victim of his circumstances.

# Serve rather than DEserve.

"Serve wholeheartedly, as if you were serving
the Lord, not people."--Ephesians 6:7 NIV

If I had a one to ten meter designed to measure how selfless you are, where would you be on the meter? On this meter, the devil is a zero and Jesus is a ten. In my high school days, I was probably a three or four. I was pretty proud of myself and thought life revolved around me. Now, after the events I will discuss in this principle, I would say I have worked my way up to a six or seven-- not every day, but hopefully most days.

We are all sinners in need of a Savior. I always loved when Pastor Wray did a baptism; he would say, "You won't need to teach this kid how to sin. He comes by that naturally. You will need to teach him to be Christ-like."

I have found that when I get cranky, it is usually because I feel like I am getting the short end of the stick and not being treated properly. I start to have an attitude that I deserve things, but if I can wake up every day looking for somebody to serve, I won't be disappointed.

My poor kids have only been to Disney World twice; they deserve better.

This phrase, "serve rather than deserve," came from a Jim and Shirley Dobson devotional, *Night Light*, which was a big influence in changing my attitude and moving me a couple of points up the meter. In this devotional, the Dobsons tell the true story of a fighter pilot named John Ferrier who was taking part in an air show. His engine had failed, and the plane was going down. He had a choice to make. He could bail out and save himself, but then he wouldn't have any control over where the plane crashed. It could plow into the crowd that was gathered or maybe into a nearby house. To avoid that risk, the pilot chose to go down with the airplane. He didn't deserve to die that day, but he was willing to give his life in order to save others. The devotional finishes the story like this:

> "A bunch of us were standing together, watching the show" an elderly man with tears in his eyes told Coomer. "When the pilot started to roll, he was headed straight for us. For a second, we looked right at each other. The he pulled up right over us and put it in there."
>
> In deep humility, the old man whispered, "This man died for us."
>
> A few days after this tragic accident, John Ferrier's wife, Tulle, found a worn card in his billfold. On it were the words "I'm Third." That simple phrase exemplified the life--and death--of this courageous man. For him, God came first, others second, and himself third.
>
> True to his philosophy, John Ferrier sacrificed his life for the people he had never met. If you ever found yourself in a similar situation, would you do the same?

. . .

For the sinful nature desires what is contrary
to the Spirit, and the Spirit what is contrary to
the sinful nature.--Galatians 5:17 [NIV]

That sinful nature we talked about yesterday often rears its head in the form of the thought *I deserve more*. It leads us to demand the best deal, the lion's share, the most credit, and the finest everything. From earliest childhood, as we have seen, our impulse is to focus on ourselves and to disregard the needs of others.

And, yes, this "I-deserve-it" attitude can permeate marriages. Resentment can build over who works the hardest, who spends more than his or her share of the money, and who is not doing enough to serve the other. Anger then erupts over insignificant irritants that bubble up from the cauldron of emotions. Many fights in marriage begin with the belief that we're being cheated in the relationship.

Beware of this trap. The minute we begin thinking that we are entitled to more, we've started down the slippery road to selfishness. It can devastate a relationship.

John Ferrier didn't deserve to die in an Ohio neighborhood--but when crisis came, he chose to sacrifice for others. Jesus didn't deserve to be nailed to a wooden cross--but out of love for the Father and for us, He allowed Himself to be crucified. This kind of sacrificial love seeks to serve, not "deserve"--and that changes everything!

There is a line in the movie *The Rookie* (yes, another baseball movie), where the wife tells Jimmy Morris, "I guess a girl could have done worse." That line has often come up in discussion with my wife Suzanne. She, too, could have done worse, but as a husband I could sometimes do better. It just amazes me how

I will come home with an attitude of wanting to serve her, but when she fixes me a nice dinner I can't seem to get my butt back out of the chair. Sometimes, I come home still in work mode. I am focused on the next day's work, when I should be focused on her.

It has always been a bit difficult for us because of her job working with kids. She doesn't get much adult conversation during the day, so she wants to talk in the evening. I, on the other hand, get my fill of adult conversation at work and would prefer to come home and not have to listen anymore. Then I hear myself say, "I 'deserve' some quiet time," and I realize, "Oh no! Principle #8!" The sinful nature is to want people to serve us, and we all do need times of rest to rejuvenate ourselves. However, "It's not going to be that way with you. Whoever wants to be great must become a servant."--Mark 10:43 MSG

In *The Purpose Driven Life*, "Day 33: How Real Servants Act," Rick Warren states:

> We serve God by serving others.
>
> The world defines greatness in terms of power, possessions, prestige, and position. If you can demand service from others you've arrived. In our self-serving culture with its *me-first* mentality, acting like a servant is not a popular concept.
>
> Jesus, however, measured greatness in terms of service, not status. God determines your greatness by how many you serve, not how many people serve you. This is so contrary to the world's idea of greatness that we have a hard time understanding it, much less practicing it.
>
> Thousands of books have been written on leadership, but few on servanthood. Everyone wants to lead; no one wants to be a servant. "And if anyone gives even a cup of cold water to

one of these little ones who is my disciple, truly I tell you, that person will certainly not lose their reward."--Matthew 10:42 (NIV)

Your greatness as a leader will not be determined by how much power you accumulate. It will be determined by how much you serve and sacrifice for others to help them become great. Great leaders don't succeed because they are great. They succeed because they bring out the greatness and others. I believe you have to have an ego to want to be great, but ironically, you must give up your ego and serve others in order to be great. To become a great leader, you must be a servant leader. Only through service and sacrifice do you become great. You must serve in order to lead.

In John 13:1-7, we see an amazing story of Jesus washing the disciples' feet. It occurred just before the Last Supper, as Jesus was preparing to do His biggest service of dying on the cross for us. When we say that someone is high and mighty, we usually get a picture of someone sitting up on a throne, but Jesus was certainly different; He was willing to stoop down. This washing of the feet was a huge display of humility on Jesus' part.

Walking in sandals on the dusty roads of Israel made it imperative that feet be washed before a group meal, especially since people reclined at a low table and feet were very much in evidence. When Jesus rose from the table and began to wash the feet of the disciples in John 13:4, He was doing the work of the lowliest of servants. The disciples must have been stunned at this act of humility, that Christ should wash the feet of His disciples, when it was their proper work to have washed His. But when Jesus came to Earth, He didn't come as the traditional king, but as the Suffering Servant of Isaiah 53.

In Matthew 20, the mother of two of the disciples is asking

for a special place in Heaven for her boys. The other disciples aren't sure what they think of that. Jesus responds in verses 26 through 28 NIV, "Whoever wants to become great among you must be your servant and whoever wants to be first must be your slave--just as the Son of Man did not come to be served, but to serve, and to give his life as a ransom for many."

In John 13:8 NIV, Jesus says to Peter, "Unless I wash you, you have no part with me," prompting Peter, whose love for the Savior was genuine, to request a complete washing. Then Jesus explained the true meaning of being washed by Him.

If we jump down to verse 15, Jesus tells them, "I have set you an example, that you should do as I have done to you." Jesus is the 10 on our meter. We should seek to be like Him, though we are never going to get there. Be that as it may, if you want to see God smile, serve someone.

When I do my class on serve rather than deserve, I start out with a YouTube video from Dan T. Cathy, President and COO of Chick-fil-A. In this video, he talks about the service that you receive when you are in a high quality restaurant. They go out of their way to make you feel extra special. Dan uses a side towel as a symbol of this sort of service. Imagine a waiter dressed in a tux with a towel over his arm, ready to be of service. I follow that up with a video from comedian Michael Jr. In one of his *Break Time* videos on YouTube, he talks to a variety of people in the crowd about how they are of service in the jobs that they perform. He finishes the video by asking, **"Where do you wear your napkin? Underneath your chin, waiting to be served? Or over your arm, waiting to be the servant?"**

This appeared in the Decatur *Herald & Review* in March of 2010. It was my response to being asked how I envisioned Decatur.

> I envision a Decatur that is known as the service capital of the world.

I had the privilege of representing Decatur when it was known as the softball capital of the world. The first women's Olympic softball team had strong ties to Decatur. New Zealand kids used to grow up dreaming of playing here. When we travelled to Prince Edward Island, Nova Scotia and Palm Springs, Calif., Decatur was always the talk of the softball world. Even Hector Torres defected from Cuba for the chance to pitch here in Decatur.

What else is Decatur known for? On a city data Web site [City-Data.com], a Chicago man [Drover] was quoted, "Decatur is a medium-sized rust belt city. It has seen better days since industry went overseas and/or became mechanized. What remains is a tired old city without a particular sense of purpose."

Somehow, we have become a society that thinks we deserve things. We deserve a good education, a good job, a nice house and a new car. Today, our government even says we deserve free health care. One way to differentiate Decatur is for us to become a town that is focused on serve, rather than deserve.

A hundred years ago, most jobs had to do with the farming industry. Today, only 2 percent of jobs do. Just like we had to adjust to this change in work style, today we have to adjust to an environment where most jobs are service related. If Decatur can become known as a city that is here to do whatever it takes to be of service, it would be our best bet for attracting quality companies and becoming a vibrant city with a vision.

> I would love to see every sign in Decatur display "We are here to serve you," and then prove it.

We really need to address this deserve rather than serve attitude in the church. If you are a member of a church, do you expect that church to serve you, or are you there to serve it? In reality, it should be both. The church should feed into you, but you shouldn't be a dead sea. You need to then feed it into others.

I would guess that a majority of people show up on a Sunday for selfish reasons. If that is you, the church is here to help. **If you are spiritually thirsty, the church has some spiritual water for you.** Showing up for personal reasons sure beats not showing up, but **at some point, you have to become a disciple of the church. A disciple is not a spectator. A disciple is called to participate in ministry.**

As a Christian, 1 Peter 3:15 reminds you that you should be prepared to defend your faith. You should be committed to learning the Bible. You should be committed to serving your community. You should be committed to the Great Commission to go and make disciples of all nations, including the one that you live in.

In 2005, I was asked to speak when we were having a joint service at the Lutheran School. At that time, we had services at the local community college and a variety of services at our Wood Street location, so it was quite exciting to get the entire 1,000 plus congregation all under one roof.

I started with a few questions:

> Do you major in the minor things?
>> Are you willing to "go public" with your faith?
>> Do you trust God's abundance?
>> According to our mission statement, Pastor
> Wray Offermann's vision as the coach of our Saint

Paul's team is to grow committed, passionate disciples who minister daily to our unchurched friends in the Decatur area. We will love them into a mature relationship with Jesus through relevant worship, Bible teaching and small group study. WBGL Radio has a similar vision, and I love how they say it: "So all will know Him and those that know Him will know Him more."

Have you ever seen this book called *Good to Great*? Those of you in the back have probably still never seen it! It says one of the hardest things to do is take something that is good and make it great. It says enduring, great companies (and churches) preserve their core values and purpose, while their business strategies and operating practices endlessly adapt to the changing world.

Pastor Wray doesn't have us do this stuff to be a megachurch. His ideas of new and different ministries are not to satisfy his own ego; he is trying to take us from good to great.

I am not sure if any of you have noticed this, but Pastor Wray is not as young as he used to be; with all his talents, he can only minister to so many people. If we are going to go from good to great, it is up to all of us to do the work of ministry.

Do we need a great church?

In Kent R. Hunter's *Discover Your Windows* book, it says, "The world at its worst needs the church at its best." This book calls for you not to be members of this church. This book calls for you to be a disciple of this church. Think about disciples in the Bible. Disciples aren't spectators. Disciples are equipped to do the work of ministry.

So I ask each and every one of you: What is your ministry, and how are you going to equip yourself to do it?

This isn't a very original thought, but ask not what your church can do for you; ask what you can do for your church.

God has not gifted us all the same way as He has gifted Pastor Wray, but we learned in the *40 Days of Purpose* that God has a plan for each and every one of us. Are you letting God fulfill that plan?

What is it that you do well?

What is it that you have a passion for?

How do you use that to benefit the church and accomplish the Great Commission?

Look around for a minute at all the people here. Could you imagine if we were all on the same page, working together for the good of the team, if everyone here could reach "just one more for Jesus?" We are going to need a pretty big roof to cover that group!

You need first and foremost to be committed to serving your family. I love how Pastor Rob Rienow addresses this on the Visionary Family Ministries website [non-standard use of "disciple" as a verb present in original]:

Rob's life dramatically changed in 2004. God brought him to a place of deep repentance over the fact that he was discipling other people's children, but not his own. He was a spiritual leader at church, but passive with his family. Through that time of repentance, God turned his heart to the ministry of his children and his wife. God then led him and Amy to launch Visionary Family Ministries, a ministry designed to inspire parents and grandparents to disciple their children, to help couples create mission-driven marriages and equip churches to build Bible-driven ministries. Their mission is to build the church through a global reformation of family discipleship.

When you look at things like the women's movement, you know that some good things have come out of that. Women are incredibly valuable, but should the goal be for them to be equal to men? A woman deserves equal pay to a man for doing equal work, but we can't get to the point where a woman's career becomes more important than her commitment to family. Before you get too excited, let me also say a man needs to have this same approach. His family needs to be more important than his work. Yes, he has to financially support his family, but that cannot be at the expense of his focus on his family's spiritual development.

## My Mother-in-Law

A great example of what I am trying to accomplish in this book is my mother-in-law. In today's age, the family always seems to take a back seat. That was never the case for Irma Storck. Her life was her family. Her focus was serving her husband and her three kids.

She did that in an 800 square foot home. She had to go outside to dry her clothes, and that was for the time frame that I knew of her life, starting in 1987. She was always the last one to eat and the first one to do the dishes.

We are called to go and make disciples of all nations. Mrs. Storck did that by pouring into her kids, in keeping with the first statement made in this book from Andy Stanley: "Your greatest contribution to the kingdom of God might not be something you do, but someone you raise." We should first and foremost be missionaries to our families before we worry about what is going on in the rest of the world.

1 Peter 4:10 NIV: "Each of you should use whatever gift you have received to serve others, as faithful stewards of God's grace in its various forms."

## My Mom

Almost all of us love our mommies. I am no different. My mom had a big servant's heart. Her best reward was a pat on the back and to be told that she did a job well. She and Eunice Kerwood were known as the "card ladies" at church. When my mom died in 2005, it was discovered that she had been sending out up to fifty cards a month to encourage people and recognize their birthdays. She had a plastic file cabinet that was full of cards, organized into various drawers.

My mom spent most of her life in food service. In her retirement, Mom was still in charge of bagels and donuts on Sunday mornings at the church. Pastor Wray spoke at her funeral about her always having a cup of coffee ready for him when he arrived on Sundays. My family honored her after her death by using the memorial money from her funeral to buy some new coffeemakers and coffeepots at the church.

One of the best tributes to my mom came from the Decatur Pride yearbook, in the year that she retired from the booster club board. It said:

> Verna Minton began working with the Decatur Softball booster club when it was restructured in 1980. Verna became a board member in 1988, and in most recent years served as secretary and treasurer. She and Ken have two talented

sons, Rick and Jim, who both played on the ADM and Decatur Pride teams. When a job needed done, you could always count on Verna to be there to see that it was done. In her very dedicated way, she hung right in there to see it through to completion. When people around her expressed negative thoughts or feelings, Verna always remained positive, and would frequently say, "Think positive! Things will get better and tomorrow will be a better day, just hang in there."

Our organization is a better one because of her tireless efforts over the years. She will be truly missed, but we wish Verna and her family well as she changes the course of her life to allow more time for them. Verna, from all of us a great big thank you, and we love you.

P.S. We will miss your cobblers at the ice cream stand.

Philippians 2:5-8 NIV:

In your relationships with one another, have the same mindset as Christ Jesus: Who, being in very nature God, did not consider equality with God something to be used to his own advantage; rather, he made himself nothing by taking the very nature of a servant, being made in human likeness. And being found in appearance as a man, he humbled himself by becoming obedient to death--even death on a cross!

Let's work together to turn that service meter up a couple of notches!

# Prepare yourself for opportunities.

*Whatever you do, work at it with all your heart, as working for the Lord, not for human masters ....*
*--Colossians 3:23 NIV*

*LUCK: **L**abor **U**nder **C**orrect **K**nowledge--Anonymous*

*Remember, if you fail to prepare you are preparing to fail.--Rev. H. K. Williams*

*Hard work beats talent, when talent doesn't work hard.--Tim Tebow (quoting Tim Notke)*

*I believe luck is preparation meeting opportunity. If you hadn't been prepared when the opportunity came along, you wouldn't have been lucky.--Oprah Winfrey*

When I was young, I had a bit of an ego problem. I thought everyone was paying attention to me. When I was catching in a baseball game, I thought everyone who attended the game was there to watch me and was keeping an eye on my every move. While this wasn't a very good Christian attitude, it produced some pretty good results.

In catching, there is something known as the pop time. An average base stealer takes 3.5 seconds to get from his lead at first to steal second base. The pitcher usually delivers home in about 1.5 seconds. That means that the catcher has 2.0 seconds from the time the pitch hits his glove to get the ball to the second base bag, in order to throw the attempted base stealer out. I was pretty good at this. In a goofy way, I got much better at this because of my ego. In my brain, the people who were attending the game were there because they had heard about my ability to throw the ball to second base. If they had not, then it was up to me to show them that they should be paying attention, so every chance I got, I put maximum effort into my throws down to second base as a catcher.

Heading into my senior year of high school, I was blessed to get to work out with Matt Tyner. Matt is from Decatur and walked on at the University of Miami in Florida, where he went on to be a star player, leading them to the College World Series. Because of this connection, Miami was willing to pay a bit of attention to me. I got a handwritten letter from one of the coaches at Miami, asking me to fill out a financial aid form for the school. The letter also stated that they determined scholarship money based upon how high someone went in the major league baseball draft. I think they were just doing a favor for Matt, but to read the letter, it looked like they were very interested in me and thought I was getting drafted. I took this letter and sent it to other schools. One of the schools whose attention I got was Georgia Southern. They were rivals with Miami at the time, and if Miami was handwriting someone a letter, they were interested.

Again due to my ego, I was just sure that I was going to go south to play college baseball, and Georgia Southern seemed like a good possibility. As I was getting ready to start my senior season, there was a six-inch snowfall in Decatur on Friday, when our first game was on Monday. Since it appeared our first game wasn't going to happen, my mom and I drove sixteen hours to Statesboro, Georgia, so I could look around the campus. (Unfortunately, the team did end up playing, and I missed the first game.)

I was told that I would have an opportunity to work out with the team, but I don't know that I really thought of it as a tryout. I swung the bat pretty well during the batting practice, but I couldn't get the ball over the fence. A few were hitting the wall, but I thought if they were going to be interested in a guy to play at a Division 1 college, he should be able to get some balls over the fence.

Then it came time for catching and to show them my pop time. I was only going to have a few throws to show them what I could do. There were several coaches watching, plus a bunch of Georgia Southern players. It seemed as if all eyes were on me.

I had been here before, of course. Because of my goofy mindset, I always felt like everyone was watching me anyway. Therefore, I didn't feel the tremendous pressure of the moment. This was my chance to fulfill one of my childhood dreams. This was my chance to earn a college baseball scholarship, but in my mind, I felt that I was ready. I had put in the work. It didn't faze me that this time everybody really was watching me.

All five of my throws went pretty well. However, I wasn't sure if it was good enough. As we walked away from the field, I was walking with Gary "Sarge" Harrison, who was the main coach in my recruiting. He asked, "Jim, do you know what your pop time is?" At this point in my life, I really didn't know what a pop time was, and I hadn't learned all the details about it that I told you earlier.

Sarge explained to me about a 3.5 second base stealer, the average pitcher and what a good catcher needed to do. He then told me, "Jim, we had you throwing the baseball down to second base in 1.9 seconds. Those are Marty Pevey kind of numbers." Sarge went on to explain who Marty was and that he was expected to go high in the major league draft. He then said, "I will need to talk with the other coaches, but I am thinking that we are going to want you to be the one to replace Marty and be the next catcher here at Georgia Southern."

**I was prepared for the opportunity**. My dream was to be a Division 1 college baseball player at a school in the South. While I may have had a goofy mindset that helped me get there, I also had worked very hard to prepare for my chance on the big stage. When I got my chance, I passed the test.

(Marty did get drafted and eventually made it to the major leagues. As of 2018, he is the manager of the Iowa Cubs, the Chicago Cubs' Triple-A affiliate.)

How did my collegiate experience continue, you may wonder? You will have to read other places in this book to put that all together.

As Kurtis was growing up as a catcher, I told him this story. Confidence is a big part of being a good athlete, but there is a fine line between cocky and confident. I probably crossed that line when I was a high school player. I often told Kurtis, though, that when you make your warm-up throws to second base between innings, you have to feel and act like everyone is looking at you-- because you never know when somebody actually will be watching!

One day, Kurtis was at a tryout camp at Southern Illinois University Edwardsville. It had rained that day, and the camp was delayed for several hours. When they were finally able to resume, they decided to do pop times first, and Kurtis would be the first to throw. He fired the ball down to second, and the coach said, "1.9," almost acting as if his stopwatch hadn't worked on the first throw. Kurtis' second throw was again 1.9. When Kurtis was done with his three throws, the head coach hollered at him to come into the third base dugout. He was impressed. Kurtis was prepared for his opportunity, as well.

Colossians 3:23 NIV says, "Whatever you do, work at it with all your heart, as working for the Lord, not for human masters…." **There is always someone watching.** Coach Wooden states in his *Leadership Game Plan for Success*, "Be more concerned with you character than with your reputation. Character is what you really are. Reputation is what people say you are. Character is more important." In high school, I was certainly a character, not always a person of character, but since then, God has really worked on me to shape me. We can slip things by people here on Earth, but we can't get things by God. Most people act differently if they know they are being watched. We should always have that attitude, because God is always watching.

In Galatians 1:10 MSG, Paul says, "Do you think I speak this strongly in order to manipulate crowds? Or curry favor with God? Or get popular applause? If my goal was popularity, I wouldn't bother being Christ's slave."

## PURPOSE

In his book *The Purpose Driven Life* on "Day 8," Rick Warren writes that we were planned for God's pleasure. Anything we do that brings pleasure to God is an act of worship. Worship is not just for a church service. We are told in Psalm 105:4 BBE, "Let your search be for the Lord and for his strength; let your hearts ever be turned to him."

The movie *Chariots of Fire* tells the story of runner Eric Liddell, who ran to glorify God and became an Olympic gold medalist for Great Britain in 1924. Be sure to look up his amazing story or watch the movie. One of Liddell's best-known quotes from the movie is, "I believe God made me for a purpose, but He also made me fast! And when I run, I feel His pleasure."

According to the National Center for Education Statistics, during the 2013 to 2014 school year, this country spent $634,000,000,000 (that's $634 *billion*) on public education. I am not sure what all is factored into that number, but any way you look at it, that is a lot of zeros. It breaks down to $12,509 per student. If a child goes "K through twelve" (kindergarten through twelfth grade), that means we have spent $162,617 to educate that student. Why would we spend that kind of money? It's to prepare our kids for opportunity.

It's not in the scope of this book, but are we getting our money's worth? The latest and greatest idea is that we need to go "P through sixteen" (preschool through four years of college). That would put the total spent to over $200,000.

If you're a freshman in high school and wondering why you have to learn all that stuff, it is to prepare you for the opportunities ahead. **"Failing to prepare is preparing to fail."** This was another of the many quotes that John Wooden loved to use. It is often attributed to Ben Franklin, but the Reverend H. K. Williams appears to be the first to put it in print in 1919. It's important that you think about the future and have a plan in place on how to get there. If you want to be a nurse, you need to be good at biology, so you better make sure you are taking some tough biology classes.

Proverbs 22:3 NLT says, "A prudent person foresees danger and takes precautions. The simpleton goes blindly on and suffers the consequences."

I was in McDonald's one day and overheard a kid who was interviewing for a job. He said that he had just moved back to Decatur, Illinois, from Mississippi, where he lived with his dad. He was coming back here for his senior year of high school and to live with his mom. The interviewer asked him which high school he was going to attend. The kid wasn't sure yet; he had heard that both coaches were pretty good. The discussion then turned toward basketball. After a while, the interviewer got back on task and asked the kid what he planned to do in the future. He replied, "I still have a dream of playing in the league [NBA]."

I hate to burst that kid's bubble, but as I evaluated his situation, I was pretty sure he was not NBA material. If you are six foot, two inches tall and they don't know about you heading into your senior year of high school, the odds are not in your favor.

If I were to have a conversation with that kid, first of all I would not trash his dream. We don't want to get in the business of telling kids they aren't special, because they are. It just may not be special in a "playing in the league" sort of way. It can be good to set high goals, but it is important to be realistic about the amount of effort that it is going to take to get there. Let's make sure we have a plan B and C. We need lots of teachers, CPAs and store managers. Which job do you want to shoot for at this level?

It is very important that our educational system helps kids get a realistic view on life. In an interview with TheBestSchools.org, Ben Carson made this point quite clearly:

> You've got so many of these young boys running around--for instance, in the inner city--thinking that they're going to be the next Michael Jordan, or the next Michael Jackson, or somebody. I mean, if you can do that, and people are paying you millions and millions of dollars, "Why do I need to bother with algebra, grammar, all this stuff? I don't need to do that. I can buy and sell any school that I want." But what they don't realize is only seven in one million will make it as a starter in the NBA. One in ten thousand will have a successful career in entertainment. So, your odds are not very good. Less than one percent of people who go to college on an athletic scholarship end up playing professional sports — and if you do end up playing, your average career span is three and a half years. So, we need to reorient people in terms of what real success is all about.

In his role as Secretary of the Departmanet of Housing and Urban Development (HUD), Ben Carson hopes to achieve this reorientation through a network of "EnVision Centers" throughout the urban areas of the U.S. According to the HUD website, these EnVision Centers will accomplish this through a four-pillar program:

> The Economic Empowerment pillar is designed to improve the economic sustainability of individuals residing in HUD-assisted housing by empowering them with opportunities to improve their economic outlook. The Education pillar seeks to bring educational opportunities directly to HUD-assisted housing and includes partnering with public and private organizations that approach education in non-traditional ways on non-traditional platforms. The Health and Wellness pillar is designed to improve access to health outcomes by individuals and families living in HUD-assisted housing. The Character and Leadership pillar is designed to enable all individuals and families residing in HUD-assisted housing, especially young people, to reach their full potential as productive, caring, responsible citizens by encouraging participation in volunteer and mentoring opportunities.

It is very important that you help your kids think about how they are going to make a living and then make sure they have a plan in place to accomplish that.

I have enjoyed hearing J. J. talk about his experiences in freshman basketball. The four years of high school seem to be a little more meaningful than most of life. The Fellowship of Christian Athletes (FCA) focuses on this period of a person's life. This is the time when you begin the transition from being a kid to being an adult. You are moving from being under someone else's roof to the point where you will have your own roof. High school and college can set the tone for how the rest of life is going to go.

Sometimes a coach gets the six-two kid who has always been a lot bigger than his classmates. He is used to being the man in the middle on the basketball team, where he can use his size to a big advantage. However, he is probably done growing. If he is going to be the man in the middle on the varsity team, he needs to be six-five, and when his parents are both under six feet tall, the odds of that happening aren't very good. You need him to help your freshman team, but you also need to help him begin to expand his game, if he is going to be a varsity player.

## CAREER

Some people have the pleasure of working in the family business. If you grew up on a farm, you're probably pretty well prepared to be a farmer yourself and continue in the family business, if you so desire. I think of a person I know whose dad was the general manager and part owner of a car dealership. When it came time for the father to cut back, his son was groomed to take over the position. Some of us are blessed in that way, while some of us are not.

Why do we see so many professional athletes have children that become athletes as well? Is it something that is in their genes? Are they born with more ability than others? Or do the kids become professional athletes as well because they understand the work ethic that is needed to be successful?

Stephen Curry has been a very successful player for the Golden State Warriors. He is an interesting example to look at. As Scott Davis explains in an article for *Business Insider*, his dad, Del Curry, was a long-time NBA player, but when Steph was fourteen, he was very small. He was a very good shooter, but he had to shoot from his hip to get the ball all the way to the basket. As a freshman in high school, he had to learn to shoot differently if he was going to be able to play at a higher level. Typically, when most athletes get to the point where the game is no longer easy for them, they begin to break down and give up. What was it that allowed Steph to work through this tough time in his life? Was it talent? Was it desire? Was it confidence to continue to believe in his dream?

It is hard to say that it was all about genes, when you look at the fact that small Davidson University was the biggest school that would take Steph out of high school because of his small stature. However, Steph continued to get bigger and worked very hard to become a magical dribbler, shooter and scorer.

In 2017, my grandson Noah is four years old. He is small for his age, so he appears to be even younger. People rave about his ability to play baseball, but that is what Noah does, because that is what Mintons do. We are ballplayers. Noah's dad, J. J., spends time with him playing the game. When he comes to his papa's house, it usually doesn't take long before we are out in the backyard playing some ball.

It also doesn't hurt that people give Noah positive feedback. That adds to his desire to want to continue to work at it. He comes by his skill naturally, but he also puts time and effort into it. It is important that if we have a big dream, we also have a plan B or C.

How else can we get prepared to make a living?

I hate to think about how much money I have spent on my kids for them to get an education. J. J. graduated from Eastern Illinois University with a degree in Sports Management. It was one of the less expensive state schools, but there wasn't much in the way of scholarships. Kurtis went to a tuition high school, Saint Teresa, to get me warmed up for paying for Olivet Nazarene University. We were blessed that Kurt worked very hard and received some very nice academic and athletic scholarships. Emily went to the Lutheran School, which was also a tuition high school. She then headed off to Illinois State University.

There is a big push to get every kid into college now. How about having them learn more in high school? How about having them come out of high school prepared to have a good job? I realize this gets harder as technology takes some jobs away, but there should be somebody that can design a program where for $160,000 a person can establish some sort of career.

In a speech dated December 4, 2013, Barack Obama said, "A child born into the bottom 20 percent has a less than 1-in-20 shot at making it to the top. He's 10 times likelier to stay where he is." That is often attributed to lack of opportunity--and I am sure that is a big part of it--but how much of it is also lack of a good mentor to show the child the needed work ethic?

Some people see the Bible as just an ancient book, but I see it as God's game plan for life. I believe the family is a huge part of that game plan. It is a mom and dad teaming up on their kids to make them successful, whether they want to be or not. It requires a couple willing to provide the discipline necessary to make their kids successful. I don't believe our public schools will ever be able to succeed, until we get the family right.

## MARRIAGE

I love to hear stories of how men met their wives. (In Principle #13, I discuss how I met Suzanne.) I was talking with a dad the other day who was trying to help his daughter pick a college. We talked about how big a deal this was towards her career, but I also added that it is probably where she is going to meet her future spouse. This was a little overwhelming for the dad to think about.

I was recently talking to a guy in his mid-twenties who was very impressive. He seemed to have a very good understanding of his faith and a good grasp of life in general. He was from a good family and just a real pleasure to talk to. He was telling me that he was going down to Missouri to see his girlfriend. He had attended a Christian college, and I asked if she was someone hemet in college, thinking they might have been separated by him taking a job in Decatur. "No, we met online," he replied. For some reason, that just didn't seem right to me, but I guess if God can put you in a particular place to meet your wife, he can also put people together over the internet.

I hear some stories of people in the old days who got married pretty quickly. One buddy showed me the pictures of his wedding. They had to do it on a Sunday because he was getting shipped off to Vietnam, and they wanted to get married before he went.

If you watch the Duggar family's show, they talk about the difference between courting and dating. Mara Betsch goes into detail about the Duggars' courtship policies in an article on TLC. com entitled "8 Simple Rules for Dating a Duggar Daughter." Courting seems like a very old-fashioned approach, but I think it is a biblical approach.

Suzanne and I have prayed that our kids would meet great future spouses. We are so blessed that J. J. found Ashley and that she has meant so much to our family.

My point here is that someday you are going to meet Mr. or Ms. Right, and you don't want to be Mr. or Ms. Wrong at that time. You are going to want to put on the full-court press to try to woo them. If you don't have a career in mind, haven't taken care of yourself physically or spend most of your time in your parent's basement playing video games, you may not be in the position to make that happen.

James 4:14 NIV: "Why, you do not even know what will happen tomorrow. What is your life? You are a mist that appears for a little while and then vanishes."

Pastor Wray liked to say, "We are all terminally ill. The odds of death are pretty much 100%; at some point, we will be checking out. Make sure you are ready."

Proverbs 16:9 NIV says, "In their hearts humans plan their course, but the LORD establishes their steps." This verse makes me think of the doctor in the movie *Field of Dreams*. Archibald "Moonlight" Graham played one game with the New York Giants in 1922, but never had a turn at bat.

The lead character in the movie, Ray Kinsella, is troubled by Graham not getting an official at bat. One night, Kinsella finds himself back in 1972, talking with Graham about his baseball disappointment. Graham informs him it would've been a much worse disappointment if he didn't have his career as a small-town Minnesota doctor. That wouldn't have happened if he had achieved success in baseball.

Kinsella next meets Graham when he shows up as a kid wanting to be a ballplayer. When Kinsella's daughter starts choking on a hotdog, Graham is forced to choose between a career in baseball or as a doctor. He immediately chooses to return to being a doctor, his real purpose in life, and saves the little girl.

My point is: It may be that God will choose your purpose. I think it is important to always go to God for answers. I believe something magical happens when you get into God's Word, the Bible. Even though the original words are two thousand years old, God will speak to you as you meditate on His book. Don't look for the answer you want; look for God's will. Let Him determine your steps.

I first heard "Work like everything depends on you, but pray like everything depends on God" from Tim Tebow. I try to take that approach. I know that God is in control, but despite spending a lot of time in His Word, I am still confused over what is up to me and what is His territory.

The following story gets sent around the internet from time to time and describes this situation quite well.

A fellow was stuck on his rooftop in a flood. He was praying to God for help. Soon a man in a rowboat came by and shouted to the man on the roof, "Jump in! I can save you!" The stranded fellow shouted back, "No, it's OK. I'm praying to God, and He is going to save me." So the rowboat went on.

Then a motorboat came by. The fellow in the motorboat shouted, "Jump in! I can save you!" To this the stranded man said, "No thanks, I'm praying to God, and He is going to save me. I have faith." So the motorboat went on.

Then a helicopter came by, and the pilot shouted down, "Grab this rope, and I will lift you to safety!" To this the stranded man again replied, "No thanks, I'm praying to God, and He is going to save me. I have faith." So the helicopter reluctantly flew away.

Soon the water rose above the rooftop, and the man drowned. He went to Heaven. He finally got his chance to discuss this whole situation with God, at which point he exclaimed, "I had faith in You, but You didn't save me! You let me drown! I don't understand why!"

To which God replied, "I sent you a rowboat, a motorboat and a helicopter; what more did you expect?"

The basis for this book is all these crazy thoughts I get in my head. Often after a little research, I realize that a thought wasn't originally my idea; I'd actually heard it somewhere else and had forgotten about that, but I also pray for guidance to try and figure out what is a good idea and what is a God-idea.

## HEAVEN

Have you ever noticed that the oldest person in the world doesn't seem to live too long after achieving that designation? (I'm joking, of course!)

Ben Franklin lived to be eighty-four years old. That is pretty amazing when you realize that, according to the Mindset List of American Death and Remembrance developed by Ron Nief and Tom McBride of Beloit College for Legacy.com, life expectancy during the period of the American Revolution was about thirty-five. According to the Centers for Disease Control and Prevention (CDC), the current average life expectancy for a person in the United States is seventy-eight, so that means we will all die in our seventies, right? Unfortunately, we can't get that guaranteed. We never know what day could be our final day on Earth. In

Principle #7, I talk about Michael Collins. Thank God he was ready for Heaven when his life was cut short at age twenty-two.

Make sure you are prepared for the opportunity of Heaven. Don't say that you're going to enjoy life now and worry about God later because not everybody gets that timeline.

GotQuestions.org is a reference I use when I am looking for answers. One question I had was: What do other religions believe about how to get to their Heaven? For Islam, the website said this:

> Islam is a take-off on the Christian/Judeo God. Muslims believe salvation comes to those who obey Allah sufficiently that good deeds outweigh the bad. Muslims hope that repeating what Muhammad did and said will be enough to get to heaven, but they also recite extra prayers, fast, go on pilgrimages, and perform good works in hope of tipping the scales. Martyrdom in service to Allah is the only work guaranteed to send a worshiper to paradise.

The great thing about Christianity is that we know exactly where the line is. Romans 3:23 tells us that all of us are sinners that are separated from God. There is only one way to Heaven and that is through faith in the death and resurrection of Jesus Christ. John 14:6 NIV: "Jesus answered, 'I am the way and the truth and the life. No one comes to the Father except through me.'"

As Christians, it is important that we focus on 1 Peter 3:15-16 NIV: "Always be prepared to give an answer to everyone who asks you to give the reason for your hope that you have. But do this with gentleness and respect [I have a hard time with that one], keeping a clear conscience, so that those who speak maliciously against your good behavior in Christ may be ashamed of their slander."

I sometimes hear people say that their faith is between them and God, but if you had the cure to cancer and you didn't tell anyone, how should you be thought of?

If a person has been horrible his entire life, should he go to Heaven? We get that answer in Luke 23:43, when the repentant sinner on the cross is given a trip to Paradise. In Principle #13, I talk about how Christians aren't perfect, just forgiven. That was really a hard concept for me to grasp. I saw myself as a sinner, and I really didn't want to be on God's team. But thank God He kept recruiting me. Thank God He kept putting people in my path who led me to Him.

Jesus, with his death on the cross and resurrection, has conquered terminal illness. Death becomes a transition, as opposed to an end. That is not something to keep to yourself.

As Walt Huntley put it in his poem, "God's Hall of Fame":

> I tell you, friend, I wouldn't trade
> My name, however small,
> That's written there beyond the stars
> In that Celestial Hall,
> For any famous name on earth,
> Or glory that it shares;
> I'd rather be an unknown here
> And have my name up there.

# Respect authority.

*"Similarly, anyone who competes as an athlete does not receive the victor's crown except by competing according to the rules."--2 Timothy 2:5 NIV*

*"Sports is a great way to teach kids. It's like life on steroids." --Jim Minton*

*"Forty years ago, you were taught one thing at the home and it was reinforced in the school . . . and that is respect: respect for your parents, respect for teachers, respect for elderly, respect for women, respect for law."--Coach Lou Holtz*

Once, during a Pride game, a change-up was delivered to me that I thought was a little high, but the ump decided it was strike three. I turned around, looked him straight in the eye and said in my outdoor voice, "That was atrocious!" When I got back to the dugout, one of my teammates commented that he'd never heard me cuss before.

I am not sure that "atrocious" counts as a cuss word, and I'm pretty confident that I didn't say anything else along with it. However, I know that I wasn't very nice. (Later on, a fellow church member who was in the stands that night asked me, "How did you come up with atrocious?" I responded that I just started running through the dictionary in my brain, and that was the first word I came to.)

For the next twenty years, I watched that umpire working at my kids' games, and I would always think about this incident.

I think sports is a great way to learn about life. It's important to learn to work hard, compete hard and give it everything you have, in order to be a winner. If you don't play a game by the rules, it probably won't be much of a game. It's also important to learn that if you don't play by the rules, there are consequences.

Once again it amazes me that the Bible, written two thousand years ago, addresses this in 2 Timothy. It says you can't be a winner, unless you play by the rules.

Somewhere during my sports life, I learned to respect umpires and referees. I saw a cartoon that hit home; it said, "The trouble with umpires is, they don't care who wins." I came to realize that there was always going to be some tension, because I cared who the winner would be and the official didn't. However, I became comfortable with the fact that I had one agenda and the umpire had another.

One umpire told me that his job was to make sure the game is played safely and fairly, not to get every call right. We would all like for officials to be accurate on every call, but as long as humans are doing the job, that isn't going to happen. You aren't going to find a guy who eats carrots every day to work a fifth grade basketball game.

What do you call a game with no umpires? That is a pick-up game, not a true championship.

There are plenty of stories on the internet of fans gone wild. As Andrew Joseph reported for *USA Today*, in 2017, referee Jake Higgins made some calls in the NCAA tournament that some Kentucky basketball fans didn't like. Those fans went on the website of Higgins' full-time business, a roofing company, and posted reviews trashing his integrity. They left 885 one-star reviews, which dropped his company rating to 2.1 out of 5.0 stars.

It wasn't about Higgins' roofing abilities. The reviews were focused on his refereeing abilities and how these fans wanted revenge for calls they didn't like.

In his book, *Wooden*, great basketball coach John Wooden said, "You can make mistakes, but you aren't a failure until you start blaming others for those mistakes." You must learn to focus on the things you can control. If a referee makes a bad call, it is one thing to voice your opinion in a respectful way. It is another when you act rudely, like many people we have all witnessed.

I remember watching a coach I respect go out to argue a call. It was an important game, and two calls in a row had gone against his team. His line was, "Just once, *just once*, could we get one of these fifty-fifty calls?"

I am sure what he really wanted to say was something like: "You are blind as a bat! Don't you need a dog out here, to help you get around? I thought only horses slept standing up. Is this your cell phone? Because it has three missed calls! You call more strikes than a union delegate. You're making more bad calls than a telemarketer. Bernie Madoff has more integrity than you. You need to go back to your job as a lookout on the Titanic. Now I understand why you and the other manager look so much alike! You may not be the worst ump in the world, but when that guy dies. . . Blue, it's a strike zone, not an end zone!" (These are just a sample of what I've heard over the years.)

I had a buddy who was a college referee. He wore glasses most of the time, so the first time I saw him working, I was surprised that he was wearing contacts. I asked him about it, and he replied that wearing glasses he was just too easy a target.

I was once in a really big game for a National Championship, and the umpire got hit directly in the cup and had to leave the game. During the delay, I had an interaction with a player on the other team. He implied that their catcher missed the ball on purpose, so the umpire would get hit because they didn't like how he was calling the game.

My experience at the Lutheran School Association has been that we Christians could do a much better job of respecting the authority of the officials.

My wife and I once went to a really exciting high school basketball game between a couple of the public schools. Each team kept going on fifteen-point runs. Just when you thought one team was going to run away with it, the other team would come right back. It was an awesome game, yet what do we remember most about it? The lady right behind us who was yelling at the referee, pleading with him to be fair. During the entire second half, it was difficult to enjoy this incredible game, because of all the whining and complaining coming from behind us.

It amazes me what I hear when I go to a game where I don't care who wins. I will see some friends rooting for one team and ask them about the game. Their response is, "The refereeing has been so bad. Every call has gone against us." Later, I'll sit with someone who is rooting for the other team and ask them how things are going. Their response? "The refereeing has been so bad. Every call has gone against us!"

I hope we realize that can't be.

It has been said that the definition of insanity is doing the same thing over and over again and expecting a different result. It amazes me how people can go to game after game and focus on the people officiating the game. Yes, it would be nice if we had more accurate officiating. Yes, there are times that refs have a bad approach towards a certain team, but if you don't have refs, it is just a pick-up game. We can't have a true winner unless someone is enforcing the rules of the game.

It's crazy how sometimes we can look at a play from nine different angles, and from two or three the player looks safe while from the rest of them he looks out. At most levels, umpires don't have the benefit of instant replay; they have to call it like they see it in the moment. However, major league umpires do get graded against a computer strike zone on balls and strikes that they call, so at that level, there is an attempt to measure the quality of the officiating.

As a catcher for close to twenty years, I got to spend a lot of time with umpires. Most of them were pretty good guys. They were giving up their time to make a little bit of money and serve the game. We are hearing now about a shortage of umpires, and the day may come when that is a concern.

Sometimes, you had umpires who were having bad days or just didn't feel very well. I remember coaching one of Kurtis' games in Champaign, and the umpire was having some struggles. When I had a little discussion with him, it came out that it was his thirteenth game of the weekend. I guess he had a pretty good excuse for not being able to see straight. It's easy to say that is ridiculous, and a guy shouldn't work that many games. However, I expect his goal was to make as much money as possible for his family, so he was willing to push the limits of his capabilities.

It took me to while to realize that, just as with any other sort of communication, the best approach with an official is the honest approach. When he calls ball four on a pitch that you think is strike three, try saying, "Oh, man! I thought we had one there. You thought it stayed low, huh?" Using a discussion tone, as opposed to an insulting tone, shows you are questioning the call, not his integrity.

If a one-two pitch was on the outside corner and got called a ball, I might say something like, "Oh, that was a good pitch, maybe not a strike, but surely a good pitch."

When it comes down to winning a game, it may be difficult to get a favorable call at the end, if you have been laying into the ref on every call throughout the game. Some coaches say they are lobbying early in the game to get that call towards the end, but I can't see that happening if you have soured the ref. John Wooden (in his book, *Wooden*) said it best: "Never be disagreeable just because you disagree." That being said, in the heat of the game it is very easy to forget that.

Let's go back to the coach I mentioned earlier who said he wasn't getting the fifty-fifty calls. He disagreed with the call in a way that was less disagreeable. Instead of insulting the umpire's abilities and integrity, the coach made his point without trying to deliver a lethal blow.

After the game was over, the team wanted to complain about how the umpiring had cost them the big game. The coach would not have any of it. He said, "We are never going to blame an umpire for losing a game. We must focus on what we can control."

When Kurtis was playing basketball in high school, websites were starting up where you could log in and watch the game tape. More times than not, it appeared that the calls evened out. The official might miss a travel by the opposing team; but then later it slides by when your guy knocks the ball out of bounds, and it is awarded to your team. It is always hard when the last call goes against you, even if you have been getting the better end throughout most of the game.

Sometimes, I think it is good to expect that things are not going to go your way. That way, you are prepared when you have to overcome obstacles. If you are expecting challenges, you won't be as surprised when they happen, so you'll be ready to deal with them. As a team, you have to try not to be in a position where the umpire has a chance to decide the outcome of a game because half the time, it is going to go your way, but half the time, it isn't.

One of the most important things that we learn from this interaction with umpires is to respect authority.

Transition this to the current discussion regarding African Americans and police. It's great to expect more from the police, but I think we have to keep in mind what's been said about umpires: that no matter how hard they try, they are going to get some things wrong.

There have been times that I have gotten really upset when I have heard about the Ferguson, Missouri, story. My bias is to take the side of the police officer. As I review the facts, it seems to me that Michael Brown was prone to trouble. I don't believe the police officer woke up looking to kill someone. It also seems a real stretch when people offer a "hands up, don't shoot" analogy. Maybe Darren Wilson could have handled the situation better, but to imply that Brown was just some innocent kid seems inaccurate.

Do police need to improve? That should always be the goal, especially when I listen to black Christian leaders like Ben Watson and Representative Tim Scott, who says in an article by Louis Nelson for *Politico* that racism from the police is real.

When I look at racism, I ask, "Do we want a solution, or do we want revenge? Do we want to improve things going forward, or do we want compensation for the past?"

In God's eyes, we shouldn't see color. There is only one race, the human race. We are all descendants of Adam and Eve, or of Noah and his wife, depending upon how you look at it. Christian singers Mandisa and TobyMac teamed up on a song in 2017, "We All Bleed the Same." The song features the line: "We are more beautiful when we come together, so tell me why we are divided."

America has some ugliness in its past. Slavery was wrong. Segregation was wrong. We should try not to judge a book just by its cover.

I have often said that you could not pay me enough money to be a policeman. It takes a special sort of person to walk into the situations that they handle. They often deal with a variety of people who are not very educated and not good communicators, so I see how there can be miscommunications. Many of the policemen I know have a certain cockiness about them. To be in such a high stress position, I think you have to, just to get the job done.

As I think about this situation, I try to look at it from different angles. When emotion gets into the process, it often affects our ability to be rational.

As I was thinking about grading police, I ran across this article from NPR that says that one third of murder cases don't get solved. Those who don't like the police can use this to say they are lazy and don't care, but this article indicates that percentage hasn't changed much since the 1960s. You'd expect that with all the new technology, it would make crime-solving easier, but the article points out that you also have a mentality today where people don't want to snitch.

I would hope that no matter which side you fall on in this debate, you would take some time to think about the other side's point of view.

Ben Watson is a professional football player, who has played with the New England Patriots, New Orleans Saints and Baltimore Ravens. I view Ben as a Christian man with high character, so I value his opinion; it appears that others do, as well. During the situation in Ferguson, he posted his feelings on Facebook. In the post (reprinted in his book) Ben talked about why he was angry, frustrated, fearful, embarrassed, sad, sympathetic, offended, confused, introspective, hopeless, hopeful and encouraged. This post ended up being liked over eight hundred thousand times.

Ben followed up the post with a book titled *Under Our Skin: Getting Real about Race*. In the introduction, he writes that we need to have an open national dialogue about the hot button issues of race that affect us all. As he looks at a variety of different emotions that he feels, one (from his Facebook post) is, "I'M HOPELESS." He says that he feels hopeless because, "I've lived long enough to expect things like this to continue to happen. I'm not surprised, and at some point my little children are going to inherit the weight of being a minority and all that it entails."

But he also says, "I'M HOPEFUL, because I know that while we still have race issues in America, we enjoy a much different normal than those of our parents and grandparents. I see it in my personal relationships with teammates, friends, and mentors. And it's a beautiful thing."

Finally, Ben writes:

> I'M ENCOURAGED, because ultimately the problem is not a SKIN problem, it is a SIN problem. SIN is the reason we rebel against authority. SIN is the reason we abuse our authority. SIN is the reason that we are racist, prejudiced, and lie to cover for our own. SIN is the reason we riot, loot and burn. BUT I'M ENCOURAGED because God has provided a solution for sin through his son Jesus, and with it, a transformed heart and mind. One that's capable of looking past the outward and seeing what's truly important in every human being. I'M ENCOURAGED because the gospel gives mankind hope.

In chapter 5, "Fearful and Confused," Ben sums up some of the points that I am trying to make in this book:

> But here's a reality that many black people don't know: Somehow, some way, we have to *get over it*. We have to suck it up and obey when we are called to. We really must learn the practical value of obeying a policeman, if only to save our own skin sometimes. Otherwise, we will not win.
>
> I think the bigger problem today is the lack of respect for authority in general. Disobeying a police officer is only the tip of the iceberg. Some men and women who would defy a police officer are the same ones who bristle at instructions from their bosses at work. They are the ones who wouldn't listen to the teacher at school and who have hamstrung today's education system with few disciplinary options.

My sister, a teacher, laments the difficult time she has at school when kids are unruly and when parents seem to assume their kid could never do anything wrong. The root of this defiance is kindled in the home, where many parents, of all shades and ethnicities, are absent, detached, or simply defeated when it comes to instilling respect for authority into their children.

We live in an increasingly self-centered culture where, more and more, "we" is becoming "me." This plays out before our very eyes when we refuse to be told what to do and how to act and we preach that individuals should do what's best for them. The problem is that what's best for us is not always what we think is best for us. [Emphasis in original]

Was Dr. Martin Luther King, Jr., a man of God or a man of the world? Did he have a WORDview, as discussed in Principle #1, or a worldview? Was he a special individual, or was he another Jesse Jackson or Al Sharpton? I don't see Jesse and Al as men of God. They may carry the title of reverend, but I think they are more about personal gain than godly gain. Is Martin Luther King, Jr., in the same category or a different category? (Also, did you know that Jesse Jackson was with Dr. King when he was killed?)

I believe that Martin Luther King, Jr., was special. In one of his last sermons, he preached that he was not afraid to die. If you have a worldview, death is a very scary thing; death is the end, but if you have a WORDview, death on this earth is just part of the journey. As Philippians 1:21 NIV says, "For to me, to live is Christ and to die is gain." I think Dr. King believed this verse. If they were ever to do a Bible: Part 2, I believe this story would be in there: A man preaches that he is not afraid to die, and the next day he does. That's biblical stuff.

Yes, Martin Luther King, Jr., did struggle with the flesh, like we all do. David was considered a man after God's own heart, and he had many of the same shortcomings. I would encourage you to research the sermons of Dr. King.

At the time I was researching this topic, Dabo Swinney made some comments at a press conference that I thought showed a tremendous example of Christian character. Swinney, football coach at the University of Clemson, was asked to comment on Colin Kaepernick's protest of not standing up for the national anthem. This was during the time that Barak Obama was President, and the government was doing everything possible to separate the church and state. I thought Coach Swinney's entire ten-minute "sermon," as some in the press called it, was one of the best commentaries on this situation.

Swinney was a walk-on football player at Alabama who made himself into a great football coach. In a YouTube video posted by ESPN Player, he tells an interesting story about how his mother lived with him in a college apartment after his parents divorced. He has been bold in sharing his faith, and, as the organization's website reports, he is a big supporter of the Fellowship of Christian Athletes.

In the YouTube video of his "sermon" (posted by EBC), Coach Swinney starts out by saying that people have the right to protest in this country, but he thought that what Kaepernick was doing was creating more divisiveness, not less. Notable quotes from Coach Swinney's speech include:

> "I hate to see what's going on in our country, you know. I really do. Because I think this is a good world. I think this is a great country."

> "I think one of the greatest leaders this world has ever seen was Martin Luther King. I don't know that there's ever been a better man or a better

leader. . . . He changed the world through love in the face of hate. He changed the world through peace in the face of violence. He changed the world through education in the face of ignorance, and he changed the world through Jesus."

"A lot of these things in this world were only a dream for Martin Luther King: not a one-term, but a two-term African-American president. And this is a terrible country? That was a dream for Martin Luther King. [There are] interracial marriages. I go to a church that's an interracial church. Those were only dreams for Martin Luther King. Black head coaches, black quarterbacks, quarterbacks at places like Georgia and Alabama and Clemson, for Martin Luther King, that was just a dream, just a dream. Black CEOs, NBA owners, you name it. Unbelievable."

"I think we have a sin problem in the world. . . . It's so easy to say we have a race problem . . . but we got a sin problem."

and

"The answer to our problems is exactly the way they were for Martin Luther King when he changed the world: love, peace, education, tolerance of others, Jesus."

What did people have to say about the speech that I thought was the best I'd ever heard? CBS Sports posted an article by Ben Kercheval entitled, "Swinney misses mark with well-intentioned comments on Kaepernick protest."

Shaun King, a liberal columnist for the New York Daily News titled his September 14, 2016, column "Clemson Coach Dabo Swinney's speech on injustice in America is the dumbest thing I've ever heard."

Be sure to watch this speech; you can find the video posted by EBC by searching on YouTube for "Dabo Swinney Martin Luther King."

In 2017, Swinney's Tigers won an NCAA National Championship. Rumor has it that throughout the year, Swinney used Phillipians 4:13 NKJV as the team's battle cry: "I can do all things through Christ who strengthens me." As Richard Johnson points out for SB Nation, the appropriateness of that verse was shown when number four, Deshawn Watson, threw a touchdown pass to number thirteen, Hunter Renfro, a phenomenon South Carolina native "Lindz the It Girl" interpreted as a sign from God. "[It] gave me chills," she notes in her blog. Whether or not the rumor is true, Johnson reports that Coach Swinney did recite the verse at the championship celebration at Memorial Stadium and pointed out the connection between 4:13 and the winning touchdown pass.

We have to have rules. We have to have someone enforce those rules. Are the people enforcing the rules always going to get it right? No, but if we throw the rules out the window, we end up with the Wild West.

**It is my hope that umpires get better; it is my hope that policeman get better, but the one thing that I can control is my reaction to these things. We have to work our way through our past hurts in order to respect authority. To be the best we can be we have to focus on the things that are under our control.**

Do you respect your kids? I see respect as a two-way street. Way back in Principle #1, we mentioned that rules without relationship lead to rebellion. There were a few times when I treated my kids as if they didn't deserve respect. Sometimes they would work hard and get a bad result, and I would be offended by the bad result. In the midst of showing my disappointment, I would come to realize that they did try their best, and as John Wooden says, that is success.

I love watching episodes of *The Andy Griffith Show*. He was the ultimate father to learn from. In Principle #1, I talked about the episode "Opie and the Spoiled Kid," but if you search on YouTube for "Andy Griffith life lessons," you will find some other episodes as well. In "Opie the Birdman," Opie accidentally kills a mother bird with his new slingshot. Instead of a "whoopin'," Andy opens the window and makes Opie listen to the baby birds chirping for their mother. It seems a little harsh by today's standards, but I believe Andy was always firm but fair.

Part of respect is making sure that we give our kids quantity, as well as quality, of our time. When I summarize this book, I am going to talk about teachable moments. You just never know when those are going to come up, and it is important that you are present both physically and mentally when those opportunities present themselves. If your child makes the error that loses the game, it is important that you are there to experience it with your child and subsequently to help in dealing with it. If your child gets the game-winning hit, it is important that you are there to help your child handle the success.

As we watch the rioting and protesting that goes on today, it is important that we realize good things don't come when we see ourselves as a victim, as I discussed in Principle #8. When people protest and cause destruction in demanding their rights, I often see the situation as "two wrongs don't make a right." You may have gotten a bad call, but a good man makes the best of the way things turn out and continues to seek justice through respectful means.

It always amazes me when you run into successful people whose kids could use some help. These people are respected in the community, but their kids do not respect them at home.

It is most important that we respect the number one authority: We have to respect God. I see God as complicated. In Principle #11, I talk about how if I were God, there are things I would do differently. Somehow, it doesn't seem like a great idea to tell the God of the universe that He is doing it wrong. I believe the Bible is God's game plan. It is the set of rules that we are supposed to play by in the game of life. In Principle #1, I mentioned that some people see God as a mean bully, but He doesn't set these rules as a way to harm us, but rather as a way to love us.

There are times my kids see me as very intolerant, but loving your children is not about giving them what they want. Love is about doing what is best for them. We must praise them when they are on the proper path, but we must discipline them when they get off that path.

Hebrews 12:7-11 NIV says:

> Endure hardship as discipline; God is treating you as his children. For what children are not disciplined by their father? If you are not disciplined—and everyone undergoes discipline—then you are not legitimate, not true sons and daughters at all. Moreover, we have all had human fathers who disciplined us and we respected them for it. How much more should we submit to the Father of spirits and live! They disciplined us for a little while as they thought best; but God disciplines us for our good, in order that we may share in his holiness. No discipline seems pleasant at the time, but painful. Later on, however, it produces a harvest of righteousness and peace for those who have been trained by it.

Proverbs 1:7 RSV: "The fear of the LORD is the beginning of knowledge; fools despise wisdom and instruction."

*James W. Minton, Sr. (Jim)*

Proverbs 3:7 NRS: "Do not be wise in your own eyes; fear the Lord, and turn away from evil."

Luke 1:50 NAS: "And His mercy is upon generation after generation toward those who fear Him."

# Don't lose Heaven when you are going through hell.

John 16:33 MSG: "I've told you all this so that trusting me, you will be unshakable and assured, deeply at peace. In this godless world you will continue to experience difficulties. But take heart! I've conquered the world."

**"If I were God, I would do it differently."**

**There is Heaven. There is hell. There is Earth with a little bit of both.**

I believe Heaven is the presence of God and the absence of sin. Hell is the absence of God and the presence of sin. On Earth, we can go either way. We may have periods where God is present, and there is no sin. However, in this fallen world, in our sinful bodies, we are eventually going to revert back to sin.

What does this make a place like our public schools, where they are demanding that God not be present?

Many people think Christianity is just about not sinning. You will occasionally hear people say that they are better than the Christians, because they sin less. As Christians, we should always be striving for Heaven. This means that we need to keep God present and sin absent, but on Earth, we are always going to struggle with our sinful nature. The thing that separates Christianity from other religions is that Christianity is more about what God has done for us, than about what we do for God. We will unwrap this later on in this principle.

Some would consider the first few minutes after the birth

of their child to be Heaven. It is so amazing to think that two people can come together and create another human being. There is so much love in their hearts at that moment that it can be an instance where God is present and sin is absent. Still, it doesn't take long before the baby is screaming for some service, and the parents start worrying about how they are going to pay for college.

Most of us have times when we question God. Many people don't believe in God because they don't like how He is handling things. Why do bad things happen to good people? Why do good things happen to bad people? On his show, *Real Time with Bill Maher*, the political comedian and atheist once said, "If we were a dog and God owned us, the cops would come and take us away."

In the movie *Bruce Almighty*, there is a line where Bruce says, "God is a mean kid sitting on an anthill with a magnifying glass, and I'm the ant. He could fix my life in five minutes if He wanted to, but He'd rather burn off my feelers and watch me squirm."

I can't imagine the pain of having to bury one of your kids. In the chapter for Principle #7, "Don't be a victim," I told the story of Michael Collins, who was killed by a drunk driver. A few years ago, I had to comment on a friend's Facebook page after her son was murdered. The message that popped into my head was, "There is Heaven. There is hell. There is Earth, with a little bit of both."

If I had to summarize John 16:33, it would be, "Don't lose Heaven when you are going through some hell."

Matt Holliday was a big, tough-looking outfielder for the St. Louis Cardinals. On his arm, he has a tattoo of Job 38:4 ESV/NRS/RSV: "Where were you when I laid the foundation of the earth? Tell me, if you have understanding." In an article for Beyond the Ultimate (BeyondTheUltimate.org), Holliday said, "I like the book of Job. Much of Job is about trials and struggles, but also [about] understanding that God is God and we are not. . . . We are not going to understand His ways sometimes, but we must remain faithful as Job. Job 36:26 [NIV] says, 'How great is God--beyond our understanding!'"

At times, being a professional baseball player can be a very humbling experience. It is not uncommon to go twenty or thirty at bats without a hit. At other times, you are on top of the world. You can feel like a god when forty-five thousand people show up to watch you play, many of them with your name on the back of the jersey they are wearing. Later in the article, Holliday stated, "Players [like everyone else] often feel the need for approval from other people besides Jesus. For me [now], the most important--and only--thing that really matters is Jesus accepts me."

In the Bible book of Habakkuk, the prophet has a conversation where he complains to God about how bad his country has become, saying, in effect, "How can you let people act this way? How can you allow for this corrupt leadership?" God replies that He is going to send the Babylonians to devour Israel, because of all the injustice and evil. Habakkuk responds that having Babylon rule would be even worse! (Have you ever been there, where the answer to your prayer seems to be worse than what you were praying for?)

The book of Habakkuk finishes by saying that in His time, God will defeat evil, bring justice and rescue the oppressed. The message of the book is that righteous people need to live by faith that God has a plan, and it is better than ours.

When we say that we would do things differently, we are saying that we don't trust God and His plan. Instead of trying to tell God what He has gotten wrong in our eyes, maybe we should spend our time figuring out how we can get in line with His plan and purpose for our lives. Remember Psalm 46:10 NIV: "Be still, and know that I am God."

There are lots of instances depicted in the Bible where God tested people. These were times when He asked people not to lose Heaven while they were going through hell.

Psalm 105:19 NLT says, "Until the time came to fulfill his dreams, the Lord tested Joseph's character." In Genesis 22:1, it says He tested Abraham. The Israelites are tested by their forty years in the desert. Deuteronomy 8:2-3 NIV says:

Remember how the LORD your God led you all the way in the wilderness these forty years, to humble and test you in order to know what was in your heart, whether or not you would keep his commands. He humbled you, causing you to hunger and then feeding you with manna, which neither you nor your ancestors had known, to teach you that man does not live on bread alone but on every word that comes from the mouth of the LORD.

James 1:2-4 NIV has this to say: "Consider it pure joy, my brothers and sisters, whenever you face trials of many kinds, because you know that the testing of your faith produces perseverance. Let perseverance finish its work so that you may be mature and complete, not lacking anything."

Finally, in Romans 5:3-4 NIV, Paul says, "Not only so, but we also glory in our sufferings, because we know that suffering produces perseverance; perseverance, character; and character, hope."

When I played college baseball at Saint Xavier, our coach, John Morey, was a big believer in team building. He put us through endurance tests that he knew would be difficult for the team to finish. His intent was that we would be tougher mentally and physically and would learn to work together to endure the tough times of the season. I was never a person who was built for endurance, so these practices seemed especially hard on me.

One of his favorite exercises was to make us run wind sprints. Just when you thought you couldn't run one more, he would say, "You're done, if you play at . . ." and he would name one of the other schools in our conference. Of course, we'd keep running. Then he'd say it again, listing another school's name. Some nights, he'd go through the entire conference before we could stop.

I'd ask myself, "Why does this man hate me so much?" Then

the coach would end with a speech, in which he gave us this message: "Because you have worked harder, you deserve more. You have earned the right to be a part of this team and to be a champion."

I look back at pictures from that time and realize that I was in the best shape of my life.

I love to listen to John Lennox and his Irish accent. I first became aware of John in the movie *God's Not Dead*. It's hard to pick a favorite Lennox video, but one of the best is "What makes Christianity Unique?" Be sure to look it up on YouTube. It was posted by the Veritas Forum.

To summarize, the video says that when it comes to religion, they can't all be true, because they have different views on similar subjects. When it comes to the resurrection of Jesus, there are three different views. Jews believe that Jesus died, but did not rise. Muslims believe He didn't die. Christians believe that He died and rose. They can't all be true.

The Golden Rule, "Do unto others as you would have them do unto you," is part of every religion, so that is not where religions differ. It's good that today those without Christ seem to be trying to show us that they are better at the Golden Rule than we are, but they miss the point.

Lennox points out that Jews and Muslims rely on merit to get to God. It depends on your achievements. When it comes time to be accepted or rejected in the afterlife, your good deeds will need to outweigh your bad deeds to some undetermined extent. The Christian faith is not based upon this merit system.

I can't reproduce Lennox's way of speaking and his quick little jokes, so be sure to watch the video. However, I'll mention one funny story that he tells to the group at Harvard. He says to imagine him telling his wife before they were married to read a thick cookbook, and if she could keep all the rules in the book, he would accept her. He then comments, "The secret of my marriage, ladies and gentlemen, is that . . . we accepted each other at the beginning unconditionally, and because she doesn't have to keep the rules of the cookbook, so to speak, in order to gain my acceptance, that sets her free to learn to cook."

Lennox finished by saying, "Christ is the only person that offers me the knowledge of forgiveness right here and now, so . . . **I try to live for Him NOT in order to gain His acceptance, but because . . . I already have it.** It's not based on my performance or my merit. It's based on the merit of Jesus Christ, who died and rose for me."

Romans 5:8 MSG: "But God put his love on the line for us by offering his Son in sacrificial death while we were of no use whatever to him."

Be sure to read all of Romans 5. In fact, be sure to read the entire book of Romans.

In the Lord's Prayer, we pray that God's will be done on Earth, as it is in Heaven. **We want Heaven here on Earth.** We want our lives to really be how we try to make them look on Facebook, but Heaven is our reward for surviving the struggles of Earth and not losing the faith!

As Claudia Minden Weisz put it her deeply moving poem, "And God Said No":

> I asked God to spare me pain,
> And God said, "No."
> He said, "Suffering draws you apart from worldly
> cares and brings you closer to Me."
>
> . . .
>
> I asked God to help me love others,
> as much as He loves me.
> And God said,
> "Ah, finally, you have the idea."

God's no isn't a rejection; it's a redirection.

There is a scene in the movie *Evan Almighty* where God

(played by Morgan Freeman) is pretending to be a waiter in a little diner, and He strikes up a conversation with Evan's wife. The Evan character is a modern-day Noah, who is building an ark in the middle of a suburb. His wife complains to God about how Evan is acting. God points out to her that she prayed for her husband to be at home more and interact more with the kids. That is what is happening with the ark project, but the wife could not see it because it was such a crazy concept. Answer to prayer may not always show up in the way that we expect.

In a YouTube video posted by R. B., comedian Ken Davis has a great line: "I'm not OK; you're not OK, but that's OK, because He loved us anyway." I am convinced that life is about survival. We go from test to test, pain to pain, blessing to blessing, and at the finish line, we have to have God present.

Paul tells us in 2 Timothy 4:7-8 NIV, "I have fought the good fight, I have finished the race, I have kept the faith. Now there is in store for me the crown of righteousness, which the Lord, the righteous Judge, will award to me on that day--and not only to me, but also to all who have longed for his appearing."

# Forgive.

*"To be a Christian means to forgive the inexcusable, because God has forgiven the inexcusable in you."--C. S. Lewis*

*"The first to apologize is the bravest.*
*The first to forgive is the strongest.*
*The first to forget is the happiest."*
*--Unknown*

*"But God is faithful and fair. If we admit that we have sinned, he will forgive us our sins. He will forgive every wrong thing we have done. He will make us pure."--1 John 1:9 NIRV*

What is it about your family that really irritates you?

Doing life together is hard. We are by nature sinful and selfish. We all have our quirks. Some of the time, we can see past our families' quirks. Other times, they are really annoying.

I try to have a WORDview, but often the world says they have a better option. I try to be a good winner and a good loser, but sometimes I get frustrated when things don't go my way. I try not to see myself as a victim and have a serve rather than deserve attitude. Sometimes when God is putting me through a test, I lose my focus on Heaven. It is during these times that I need forgiveness.

In his song "Forgiveness," TobyMac says, "'Cause we all make mistakes some time, and we've all stepped across that line, but nothing's sweeter than the day we find forgiveness."

Using the Bible App from YouVersion on my phone, if I search the word "forgive" in the New International Version, it comes up with 150 different verses. If anyone ever asks, "What is the Bible about," you could answer that it is about forgiveness.

Ephesians 4:32 NIV is one of those verses, and it says, "Be kind and compassionate to one another, forgiving each other, just as in Christ God forgave you."

Luke 1:77 NIV says, "[T]o give his people the knowledge of salvation through the forgiveness of their sins,[.]"

Colossians 3:13 NIV: "Bear with each other and forgive one another if any of you has a grievance against someone. Forgive as the Lord forgave you."

The worldview version of forgiveness goes like this. In a YouTube video posted by John Hopkins Medicine, Karen Swartz, MD, looks at forgiveness purely from a health perspective:

> Certainly, the healthiest thing is to forgive. I mean, there are all these studies now that are demonstrating that if you are going to have lower blood pressure or better blood flow and all these different things, it's healthier to forgive. I think that it would be better if people could view forgiveness as something they are doing for themselves. Again, it's not absolution. I think they get hung up on saying, 'If I forgive you, somehow I've forgotten, or you're not in trouble.' Forgiveness is something different, which is saying, 'I am not going to have these negative emotions consume me.' That's how I feel, I think, so forgiveness really isn't about as much the other person as it is your own process of saying, I'm moving forward.

According to his biography on Google Books, "Gerald G. Jampolsky, MD, is an internationally recognized authority in the fields of psychiatry, health, business, and education. He has published extensively, including classic bestsellers *Forgiveness, Teach Only Love,* and *Love is Letting Go of Fear.*" According to his Facebook page, he is "a graduate of Stanford Medical School and a former faculty member of the University of California School of Medicine in San Francisco." In a YouTube video posted by her network, OWN, Oprah Winfrey says he "changed my life."

In *Good-Bye to Guilt,* Doctor Jampolsky states, "I can have peace of mind only when I forgive rather than judge."

In *Love Is Letting Go of Fear,* he says, "The fearful past causes a fearful future.... We cannot love when we feel fear.... When we release the fearful past and forgive everyone, we will experience total love and oneness with all."

In the same book, he also states, "Inner peace can be reached only when we practice forgiveness. Forgiveness is letting go of the past."

I think I invented the line, "Science is the process of learning what God already knows." When I read Dr. Jampolsky, I think it may be that medicine is also a process of figuring out what God already knows.

In this day and age, we have big expectations. We expect to be treated like royalty. If we don't like the service we receive, we don't go back. If our husbands or wives aren't meeting our needs, we divorce and move on.

As I was learning about business, I found some very successful people who were good at demanding things. They expected perfection and let you know if you didn't deliver, so I went through a spell where I tried to adopt this approach. Successful people don't get pushed around, but it's hard to find the line between that and having a forgiving heart.

Any good relationship is going to revolve around the ability to forgive. Whenever you put two flawed people together, both of them are going to make mistakes. Resolving those mistakes is the key to the relationship continuing to move forward.

*"When we genuinely forgive, we set a prisoner free and then discover that the prisoner we set free was us."--Lewis B. Smedes*

Matthew West is an amazing songwriter who went to college at Millikin University in Decatur, Illinois. My family members are all big fans of Matthew. We began to follow him even more closely when a member of our church, Jacob Weidenhofer, started playing guitar in Matthew's band.

Matthew asked people to write him letters about things they were going through, which he then used as inspiration for writing songs. One such letter was from Renee Napier, who told the story of how her daughter, Megan, was killed by a drunk driver named Eric Smallridge.

This story led to Matthew West's song, "Forgiveness."

Eric was behind bars for Megan's death, but Renee also felt like she was a prisoner. She had so much bitterness and anger built up towards Eric. Eventually, however, God gave her the strength to do the impossible: She reached out to Eric and said, "I forgive you."

In a live version of the song he posted on YouTube, Matthew West quotes Eric's reply: "I can't even forgive myself, and she forgave me."

In the lyrics of Matthew's song, it says: "It always goes to those who don't deserve. It's the opposite of how you feel, when the pain they caused is just too real, takes everything you have to say the word: forgiveness."

Later on in the same YouTube video, Renee says that the moment she told Eric she forgave him was the moment that healing began for both of them.

The lyrics also say, "Even when the jury and the judge say you've got a right to hold a grudge."

Renee decided to act just like Michael Collins' family, when she chose the principle of "Don't be a victim." I can't imagine the grief of having to bury your child, but how do you get through such a terrible situation? You have to find a way to forgive.

In the YouTube video mentioned above, Matthew West says it took him two years to write the song. "I realized the reason why it was so difficult to write this song, "Forgiveness," is because it's kind of hard to live that out. That's why the words of the chorus are sung in the form of a prayer: God show me how, help me to do the impossible."

As Matthew points out in the video, thinking about forgiveness leads to some "life-defining questions." Is there somebody whom you need to grant forgiveness to? Someone whom you need to ask for forgiveness from? Something that you need to forgive yourself for?

Who makes you so angry that you lose your Christianity? We have to learn to give up that anger and forgive.

In another great video Matthew West posted on YouTube, "Forgiveness . . . Part 2 - The Rest of the Story," Renee makes an appearance at a radio station. She has no idea that Matthew has written the song for her. The deejays tell her story and play the song; Renee is overwhelmed and filled with emotion. Little does she know that Matthew is in the very next room, watching her reaction through a window. As Renee begins to express her gratitude for the song, Matthew walks in and greets her with a big hug, to her complete amazement and joy.

Renee was able to take her mess and make it into a message. She went around to high schools, telling her story of forgiveness. The message became even more powerful when she could take Eric with her.

There is an incredible video on YouTube entitled "Choices," posted by Dave Mungai. It is a perfect video for parents to watch with their kids, as they prepare to get behind the wheel of a car. It starts with the statistic that, in the U.S., every fifty-four minutes, someone is killed by a drunk driver. It goes on to tell the story of Eric Smallridge.

Eric was basically your average kid. He came from a good family and was a star on the soccer team. His brother was a sheriff's deputy. Eric was one week away from graduating college, but he made the fateful decision to drive drunk. He had done it successfully before; why would this time be any different? When the accident occurred, at first Eric didn't even think it was his fault. He was shocked to learn he had killed two girls, one of whom was Renee Napier's daughter, Megan.

Be sure to look up the song "Forgiveness" by Matthew West and all the YouTube videos that tell the story. It is quite a powerful message.

If someone throws a rock at you, human nature is to pick it up and throw it back. As I heard Ken Johnson say on his *Journey to Excellence* CD, "**Hurt people hurt people**." It turns into a never-ending struggle of trying to get even. At some point, someone has to be strong enough to stop the hurt and give up the right to get even.

In *The Purpose Driven Life*, Rick Warren says that relationships are always worth restoring. In 1 Corinthians 6:5 NIV, Paul is embarrassed by the members of the church in Corinth who were splitting into warring factions and even taking each other to court. He writes, "I say this to shame you. Is it possible that there is nobody among you wise enough to judge a dispute between believers?" If you want God's blessing on your life, you must learn to be a peacemaker.

It is important that your child learns to keep the peace by being willing to take the short end of the stick occasionally and not pitching a fit when they don't get their way. A lot of times, this revolves around being willing to forgive someone who has hurt you.

The story of Monty Williams, whose wife was also killed by an intoxicated driver, is equally amazing, not only in the fact that Monty was able to forgive, but in how quickly he was able to do it.

I first read about Monty in an article written by Dave Pond for *FCA* (Fellowship of Christian Athletes) *Magazine*. He was an NBA coach who was a man of very high character. That character was put to the test when his wife, Ingrid, was killed by an intoxicated driver. You would certainly have understood if Monty had been angry and bitter at the situation and at the driver who crashed head-on into his wife's car. Instead, Monty stepped to the podium at his wife's funeral and gave one of the most amazing displays of Christianity I have ever seen. In a "A Message of Faith, Strength and Love," posted on YouTube by the Oklahoma City Thunder, it can be seen that he asked for prayers not only for his family but also for the family of the intoxicated driver.

Monty focused on the needs of others by saying:

> I don't care what you're going through. This is hard for my family, but this will work out. And my wife would punch me if I were to sit up here and whine about what's going on. That doesn't take away the pain. But it will work out, because God causes all things to work out. You just can't quit. You can't give in. See, the Bible says Satan comes to steal, kill and destroy. And America teaches us to just numb that, and it's not true. But it is true. All you gotta do is look around you. Get outside of these walls, and you know it's true.

Earlier, I talked about how well Trevor Bayne handled winning the Daytona 500 on his first attempt. I don't think Monty Williams could have handled this situation any better. Susannah Donaldson was high on meth when she crashed into Ingrid. The Williams family has five children who must go on without their mother. For Monty to have the heart of forgiveness to ask for prayer for her family as well was amazing. Talk about having a WORDview, as opposed to a worldview, talk about understanding that life is preparation for eternity, talk about not seeing yourself as a victim, about having a "serve rather than deserve" attitude, talk about not losing your Heaven when you are going through some hell, there is no better example of all of that than that speech.

I will never forget Monty's bold pronouncement of the faith in his "Message of Strength, Faith and Love": "My wife is in Heaven. . . . We didn't lose her. When you lose something, you can't find it. I know exactly where my wife is." I have to believe God said, "Well done, good and faithful servant," to Monty that day and to Ingrid as she arrived in Heaven.

This is a really bad joke, but it makes a point. If you were to lock your wife and your dog in the trunk of your car for an hour, assuming normal weather conditions where they wouldn't have trouble surviving, which one would be happy to see you when you got back and opened the trunk?

I see some people today who are giving up on people. Dogs seem to be less easily offended. Relationships with people can get very messy. Relationships with dogs seem to be a little less so. In every human relationship there is going to be some hurt, some pain, some disappointment, but we love God by loving others. Therefore, we must work hard at our human relationships. Instead of expecting others to have the forgiveness of a dog, we must take on that characteristic ourselves.

In John 18, I am sure Jesus was hurt by Peter denying him three times. In chapter 21, Jesus is resurrected and reencounters Peter. He comes not to chastise, heap guilt, or throw condescending comments into Peter's faith. Jesus comes to restore the relationship. The initial step in restoration has Jesus offering to cook Peter some fish. Then He gives Peter the chance three times to say that he loves Him and restore the relationship.

I love the fact that the word for charcoal is only used twice in the Bible. The first time is when Peter is betraying Jesus. The second time is when Jesus cooks some fish in the process of forgiving Peter.

God invites us to tell Him how we have sinned, and He promises forgiveness. As God forgives us, we are to forgive others. Matthew 6 is where the Lord's Prayer is in the Bible. I like how *The Message* version puts it in verses 7 through 9:

> The world is full of so-called prayer warriors who are prayer-ignorant. They're full of formulas and programs and advice, peddling techniques for getting what you want from God. Don't fall for that nonsense. This is your Father you are dealing with, and he knows better than you what you need. With a God like this loving you, you can pray very simply. Like this:

I have to switch back to the New International Version for the Lord's Prayer (verses 9 through 13):

> Our Father in heaven, hallowed be your name, your kingdom come, your will be done, on earth as it is in heaven. Give us today our daily bread. Forgive us our debts [sins], as we also have forgiven our debtors [those who have sinned against us]. And lead us not into temptation but deliver us from the evil one.

Verses 14 and 15 go on to say, "For if you forgive other people when they sin against you, your heavenly Father will also forgive you. But if you do not forgive others their sins, your Father will not forgive your sins."

*The Message* puts verses 14 and 15 this way: "In prayer there is a connection between what God does and what you do. You can't get forgiveness from God, for instance, without also forgiving others. If you refuse to do your part, you cut yourself off from God's part."

We started this chapter with 1 John 1:9. John MacArthur adds some enlightening commentary on this verse in his book, *Worship: The Ultimate Priority*:

> We worship God and give Him glory when we confess our sin.... The word "*confess*" in that verse is *homologeo*, which comes from the union of two Greek words--*homo*, meaning "the same," and *logos*, meaning "expression." It literally means "to express complete agreement." Confession is fully agreeing with God about the responsibility for sin and the awfulness of it. We don't often think of the confession of sin as worship, but it is. When we confess our sins, we are humbling ourselves before God, acknowledging His holiness, experiencing His faithfulness and righteousness in forgiving us, accepting any chastisement He may give, and therefore glorifying Him. In fact, confession serves the dual purpose of being an act of worship itself and of preparing the repentant sinner to worship. Hebrews 9:14 says cleansing purifies the conscience "to serve the living God." The Greek word for *serve* in that verse again is *latreuo*, which means "worship." The purifying that takes place in confession and forgiveness is an important preparation to worship.

**Do you ever have trouble forgiving yourself?** I have a hard time forgiving myself for how I acted at J. J.'s basketball games. The worst was probably an eighth grade game at Mound Middle School. I had been to the dentist that day and could hardly open my mouth. My brother-in-law, Jerry, went with me to the game. Mount Zion had upset Mound earlier in the year. This was a regional game where their season would be over if we lost. It seemed to me that we weren't using the same game plan that we used in that win. In the last game, we had got their star player in foul trouble by taking the ball to him. In this game, we didn't seem to have that approach. I guess I decided I wanted to coach the game from the stands. I decided that I knew what was best for the team. For the rest of the game, I stood and yelled instructions. The seventh grade coach, Anthony Smith, was assisting on the bench. He stood up and just stared at me. To tell you my state of mind, Anthony is a rather large African American man. I felt no fear. I was so focused on competing in that game that I was too blind to see how stupid I was acting. After the game, he continued to stare as he walked by. I had parents from the other team whom I knew come up and make comments about how I acted. At the time, I was in my own little world. The only thing on my mind was winning an eighth grade basketball game.

I had some success as an athlete because I had a bulldog attitude. I was a vocal leader of many of the teams that I played on. I guess I struggled being the father of an athlete, since I wanted to continue to be the vocal leader. Maybe God was just preparing J. J. for the parents that he would encounter as a coach.

In 2017, as fate would have it, Anthony's son, Mark, is now playing basketball at the University of Illinois. I look forward to the opportunity to hand this book to him and ask for his forgiveness some twenty years too late.

As I write this book and try to lead programs at church, the devil often reminds me that I am not worthy. As I try to write a book about being a dad, I realize that I was THAT dad. Today, I often worry about what people thought of me as I went through this crazy stage of life. I didn't then, but I do now. The devil likes to tell me that I am not good enough.

Most people are familiar with John 3:16. In Principle #4, we talked about Tim Tebow's amazing story that revolves around this verse. Some people don't get to verse 17 NKJV: "For God did not send His Son into the world to condemn the world, but that the world through Him might be saved." Jesus didn't come to rub it in but to rub it out. Likewise, we shouldn't condemn others. Romans 5:8 NKJV says that "God demonstrates His own love for us, in that while we were still sinners, Christ died for us." God has forgiven us, and as part of that forgiveness, we need to forgive others.

If Christianity were true would you believe it?

There is a God who created the universe. He put the sun approximately ninety-three million miles away (per Tim Sharp of Space.com) in just the right spot. If it were any closer, we would burn up; any further away, we would freeze. We are deceived into thinking that it rises in the east and sets in the west, but science has now discovered what God already knew. In His brilliant design, He had the earth perfectly rotate around the sun every 365 days.

This God cares about you, knows the number of hairs you have or don't have on your head. As God looked at this earth, He said, "You know what? We need a Kurtis and Emily Minton in this world. Therefore, I am going to work it out for Jim Minton and Suzanne Storck to meet, but wait! There are a couple of things I need to fix in Jim before he meets her. We have to do something about his ego. I blessed him a little too much while he was in high school, and now he thinks that it was of his own doing. Let's put him through a few rough patches before they meet."

God also decided that this world needed you. He worked things out so that could happen. Maybe that is really hard to believe. If this is true, don't you think you should live your life in accordance with His will?

# Christians aren't perfect, just forgiven.

Why am I a Christian?

Because it is true!

As Rhett Herman reports for *Scientific American*, we are standing on a ball that is spinning at one thousand miles per hour. As Tim Sharp states on Space.com, the sun is between ninety-one and ninety-four and half million miles away, depending on the earth's position in its orbit (the time of year). If it were any closer, we would burn up; if it were any further away, we would freeze. Sharp states that the moon, on average, is just under 239,000 miles away. Despite this great distance, it tells the oceans what to do.

Have you ever considered that if you ran to the store at 6 p.m., and the next day you needed to go back at 6 a.m., that store would have actually moved twelve thousand miles? It makes me a little dizzy to think about it. You would think that it would make you a lot dizzier to spin that fast!

As the National Aeronautics and Space Administration (NASA) Goddard Space Flight Center notes on their website, Proxima Centauri is the closest star to the sun. It is 4.25 light years or 268,770 astronomical units (AU) away. (One astronomical unit is the average distance from the earth to the sun.) Using NASA's conversion factor of 5,880,000,000,000 miles to one light year, that means Proxima Centauri is 24,990,000,000,000 miles away.

I often have to remind myself of the incredible design of

our world because my sinful nature wants to take over and tell God how He is supposed to run things. If I were God, I would do it much differently. However, when you get to questioning the ability of God, you often start to question the existence of God, but when I look at the complexity of humans and the universe as a whole, I have to believe that they have a Creator.

When you look at Mount Rushmore, do you think that it had a creator, or do you think that the perfect amount of wind and rain formed a rock pile that looked just like four presidents? No, the National Park Service's Mount Rushmore website discusses how a man named Gutzon Borglum, with the help of his son Lincoln, created this major landmark. Likewise, I believe the earth has a Creator. It is too much for me to believe that this all just happened out of nothing and by chance.

There is a God; I know it isn't me or you, so who is it? When I examine all the religions, Christianity seems the most plausible.

In 2014, I was going through a rough patch. I had really lost my confidence in my ability to make decisions. Things weren't working out for me as I expected, and God seemed like a good person to blame. If we are honest, I think most of us have doubts about God. It is a difficult concept. It's hard to imagine some being that is outside of time and space. I couldn't sleep; I was waking up around 2 a.m. every morning and my mind was going a hundred miles an hour. To quiet my mind and get back to sleep, I would watch videos on my phone.

In 2016, I wrote a blog for Saint Paul's Lutheran Church about whether the internet is good or bad, a theme I discuss in Principle #5. When my kids first started using the internet, I thought it was important that I send them some good information to consume on it. I figured they would be able to find the bad stuff on their own; it would be my job to direct them to positive, Christian messages. I then tried to share these ideas with others through Saint Paul's Sunday school and a class at the Lutheran School Association, but I still had the question in my head: Is God real?

I grew up in the church and attended the Lutheran school through eighth grade, but to be honest, I wasn't paying much attention. Despite having an amazing pastor in Wray Offermann and great parents, I was pretty much focused on worldly things, with a very ME attitude.

Then, at age twenty-one, I became a dad. That was a serious wake up (and grow up) call. Suddenly, I was responsible for more than just my own life.

By twenty-four, I was divorced, and this dad thing seemed overwhelming. I went in to see Pastor Wray one day and said, "Help!" His advice was to meet a nice girl from the church. In my memory, it seems like I walked out of the office and instantly met Suzanne, but in reality it was probably a couple of weeks later. I called her and asked for Susan--That's not her name!--and asked for a date.

I really believe that behind every good man is a good woman. I think God designed it for godly men to take care of godly women, but more often than not, I think it is the woman who makes the man. That was certainly true in my case. Suzanne did an awesome job of getting me back on track and back into the rhythm of going to church, but I still wasn't listening much.

After Kurtis and Emily were born, it was full-time parenting. We got involved leading Sunday school, and I really felt a calling to be a Christian father to my kids. The problem was: I really didn't know how. I didn't know how to fight my sinful nature. I didn't have the "serve rather than deserve" attitude referenced in Principle #8.

A huge turning point occurred, however, when I read the devotional by Christian author and psychologist Dr. James Dobson that appears in Principle #8. From the day I read that devotional, I at least tried to adopt a "serve rather than deserve" attitude.

Not long after that, we had to make a decision about Suzanne going back to work. I sat in my car and prayed to God for help in making the decision. After I was done praying, I flipped on the radio, and the Christian music station came on with Jim Dobson's "Focus on the Family" program. The topic was why it is important for moms to stay at home with young children. Talk about answered prayer! We were blessed that Susie could stay home for several years with our kids. I believe a huge part of Kurtis' and Emily's success came from this time that their mom was able to pour into them.

Then a buddy asked me to play one hundred holes of golf in one day, as a fundraiser. My selfish, sinful nature kicked in, and I thought it would be an awesome thing to do, just because I love playing golf. Little did I know, this would be one of the most important decisions of my Christian life. That was because the fundraiser was for the Fellowship of Christian Athletes.

I went to the first meeting about the golf outing with great excitement. It was at the beautiful Champaign Country Club. I was looking forward to hearing the details in getting to play one hundred holes of golf in one day, but the meeting started with this muscular, tough-looking wrestling coach asking the attendees if we had a personal relationship with Jesus Christ. As we talked around the table, I was again asked, "Do you have a personal relationship with Jesus Christ?" My response? "I am Lutheran."

It hit me hard at that point that I didn't even really know what a Lutheran was, let alone have a relationship with Jesus. Despite all the great people I had been around, despite my mom's and dad's best efforts, despite attending the Lutheran school and being a Sunday school teacher, when asked this question, I just didn't know how to answer it.

I had a lot of fun raising two thousand dollars in sponsorships to play golf in the Fellowship of Christian Athletes' fundraiser, but more importantly I found Christ and discovered that He wanted to have a personal relationship with me.

It's really funny how it seemed that Pastor Wray started

preaching about this right after my experience. In reality, I am sure he had already told me that I needed to do this, probably on multiple occasions. However, I needed a different sort of Q-tip to get my ears open, so my heart could respond.

Suzanne and I started joining some small groups. Meeting Scott Roney was an important step in my faith journey. I remember being at Gary and Linda Buenting's and Gary using the expression, "Christians aren't perfect, just forgiven." I thought, "Hey, that's me! I am not perfect. If Christians don't have to be, maybe I can be one." It was then that I realized that this Christian thing isn't about how great I am, but about how great Jesus is.

In Galatians 5:19-21 NIV, Paul lists a few things that a Christian should *not* indulge in. "The acts of the flesh are obvious: sexual immorality, impurity and debauchery; idolatry and witchcraft; hatred, discord, jealousy, fits of rage, selfish ambition, dissensions, factions and envy; drunkenness, orgies, and the like. I warn you, as I did before, that those who live like this will not inherit the kingdom of God."

I was guilty of a few of these. OK, most of these.

The chapter goes onto say, in verses 22 through 26, this is how you should act:

But the fruit of the Spirit is love, joy, peace, forbearance, kindness, goodness, faithfulness, gentleness and self-control. Against such things there is no law. Those who belong to Christ Jesus have crucified the flesh with its passions and desires. Since we live by the Spirit, let us keep in step with the Spirit. Let us not become conceited, provoking and envying each other.

I wasn't acting that way, but that one little expression, "Christians aren't perfect, just forgiven," made me realize that, although I am never going to live up to the standard of perfection, I can certainly still be a Christian.

I have read stories of Martin Luther, the founder of the Lutheran church, throwing himself on the ground and pulling his hair out because he just couldn't stop himself from being sinful. In Romans 7:15 NIV, Paul says, "I do not understand what I do. For what I want to do I do not do, but what I hate I do." In the end, Luther came to realize that Christians aren't perfect, just forgiven.

I got involved with a small Bible study group on Friday mornings, and we started studying the life of David. This guy was a mess. Most people are familiar with the story of Bathsheba and the fact that he basically committed murder to get the girl. Even many of David's kids were a mess, yet David fulfilled God's purpose in his generation.

David wasn't perfect, but he was forgiven.

In this same Friday Bible study, we also ventured into *The Purpose Driven Life* by Rick Warren. The first line of the book is: "It's not about you." I found this book to be simply amazing. A great many Bible verses were used. Each day the book seemed to speak directly into my life. It told me I was not an accident.

I laugh at that a little bit because my mom and dad had four children, and I expect they thought that was a very happy little family. Then several years later, here I came. Was I an accident?

A lot of us could be considered accidents. A lot of kids come along somewhat unexpectedly into their parents' lives. Now here was this book saying that God has a plan, and each and every human being is a part of that plan. The book also asked a very appropriate question, "What on earth am I here for," which I discussed in Principle #2.

This book really helped me understand a great deal more about who God is. I find God's plans to be very complicated for my little mind. Do I live eighty years here on Earth, and that's it? Is having a high batting average in high school and going on to be part of a couple National Championship teams with the Decatur Pride my great achievement in life? Is it to see how much entertainment I can get out of the television? Was it to win a local golf tournament? He who dies with the most toys and having had the most fun wins, right?

*The Purpose Driven Life* really helped me understand that I am here to have a relationship with God. To paraphrase Ephesians 2:10 NIV, I am here to fulfill good works that God has prepared in advance for me to do. Warren's book helped me to understand what the Bible was trying to tell me.

I remember playing in a church league softball tournament after my fastpitch days had ended. It was fun to play alongside fellow men from Saint Paul's, my church. One of them, former major leaguer Kevin Koslofski, is one of my favorite people. This man is such an example in my life. I was so blessed to get to compete with him on an American Legion baseball team and later to see him play in the major leagues. He was great on a baseball field, but he is just as great as a person. At this point in our lives, in our "golden" years, we were playing some church softball together. We were having a rough game, and I came in from the outfield and said, "We can do all things through Christ who gives us strength," paraphrasing Philippians 4:13. However, it felt really uncomfortable to say, even to a group of my fellow church members and my good friend. I think that was the first time that I used a Bible verse in a public situation, and, at the time, it wasn't me.

However, *The Purpose Driven Life* really spoke to me, and it made the Bible make sense. It told me that I couldn't just be a lukewarm Christian anymore.

In the essay entitled "Christian Apologetics," appearing in *God in the Dock*, C. S. Lewis states, "One must keep on pointing out that Christianity is a statement which, if false, is of *no* importance, and, if true, of infinite importance. The only thing it cannot be is moderately important."

Up to that point in my life, Christianity had been only moderately important to me, but after reading *The Purpose*

*Driven Life* I realized that if I was going to be a Christian, I had to *be* one! I could no longer hide my Christianity under a bushel; I had to let it shine. I needed to let the world know what I had found. It was about that time that Facebook came along, and I saw that as a way for me to share my Jesus. Mark Zuckerberg developed Facebook as a way to meet girls, but God presented it to me as an easy way to share my faith with the 999 people whom I am friends with.

My mom's death was another important chapter in my life. It was then that I came up with my life's verse. At Mom's funeral, Pastor Wray preached on Luke 23:43 RSV, "Today you will be with me in Paradise." In Luke's narrative, the repentant sinner on the cross had made a mess of his life. You would guess from the story that he was selfish as a person could be, that he would do anything to be the one that died with the most toys, after having the most fun. The other criminal on the cross continued in his sin to the very end. The repentant sinner, though, realized that Jesus was a big deal, and I believe he received Paradise in return for his acknowledgement.

There in 2014, I found myself again unable to trust God. I couldn't sleep. Why had God allowed these bad things to happen in my life? I really wanted to serve Him; I just couldn't figure out how. Since I was awake, I figured I might as well watch videos.

A lot of those videos were from pastor and author Tim Keller, founder of Redeemer Presbyterian Church in New York City. Keller is a very deep thinker. So many of the people whom he addressed in those videos had a liberal mindset, and my political brain loved his reasoning.

Other videos I came across were done by Doctor Robert Jeffress, pastor of First Christian Church in Dallas. He, too, is not afraid to stand up for Christians and to mix it up in the political arena.

David Pawson is an old school Bible teacher. His videos explain the Bible in a way that makes sense, and they go into an incredible amount of detail. I don't agree with all of his conclusions, but his reflections on the Bible are thought-provoking. One thing he often mentions (in "Studying the Bible," which he posted on YouTube, for instance) is that when the Bible was first written down, it wasn't in chapter and verse; it wasn't until about 1200 AD that they were divided up, so we should be careful hopping around from verse to verse. Pawson is big on reading the Bible as a story and focusing on the big picture.

The Bible Project really helped me add to this concept. Tim Mackie and Jon Collins founded the Bible Project and work with a team of others to produce videos that tell the story of each book of the Bible. They turn each book into a five to twelve minute video, with some of the books requiring a couple of videos. This is a quick way that someone could go through the entire Bible and get the whole story in about ten hours.

I also asked the question if there were sources outside of the Bible that confirmed what the Bible was saying. One of the interesting sources I ran into was Publius (or Gaius) Cornelius Tacitus. According to the *Encyclopædia Britannica* article written by Alexander Hugh McDonald, Tacitus lived from 56 to approximately 120 AD and was considered one of the great historians of Ancient Rome. In Book 15 of his *Annals*, (translated by Alfred John Church and William Jackson Brodribb, available on Wikisource), Tacitus writes about the fire of 64 AD. A website for the PBS television program, *Secrets of the Dead*, discusses the fire in considerable detail as well, stating that it burned for nine days and destroyed two-thirds of the city. According to the *Annals*, rumors spread that Emperor Nero was actually responsible for the fire himself. The book states: "It seemed that Nero was aiming at the glory of founding a new city and calling it by his name." In an attempt to quell these rumors, Nero decided to blame the fire on the Christians.

To quote the actual text of Tacitus' book:

Consequently, to get rid of the report, Nero fastened the guilt and inflicted the most exquisite tortures on a class hated for their abominations, called Christians by the populace. Christus, from whom the name had its origin, suffered the extreme penalty during the reign of Tiberius at the hands of one of our procurators, Pontius Pilatus, and a most mischievous superstition, thus checked for the moment, again broke out not only in Judaea, the first source of the evil, but even in Rome, where all things hideous and shameful from every part of the world find their centre and become popular. Accordingly, an arrest was first made of all who pleaded guilty; then, upon their information, an immense multitude was convicted, not so much of the crime of firing the city, as of hatred against mankind. Mockery of every sort was added to their deaths. Covered with the skins of beasts, they were torn by dogs and perished, or were nailed to crosses, or were doomed to the flames and burnt, to serve as a nightly illumination, when daylight had expired. Nero offered his gardens for the spectacle, and was exhibiting a show in the circus, while he mingled with the people in the dress of a charioteer or stood aloft on a car. Hence, even for criminals who deserved extreme and exemplary punishment, there arose a feeling of compassion; for it was not, as it seemed, for the public good, but to glut one man's cruelty, that they were being destroyed.

We see here that there were Christians in 64 AD, and they were persecuted for their faith. I am not sure this account fits well with those who teach the prosperity gospel. I just see no way in a time frame without computers, without typewriters, without a printing press, that forty different authors can conspire together to write the sixty-six different books of the Bible. I believe they were God inspired.

I reviewed multiple videos from the reality TV show *Duck Dynasty*. I think God has a sense of humor: Here we are, in need of a good example of the Christian family, so God gives us *Duck Dynasty*! Phil Robertson, patriarch of the clan, did give us some good messages, though. One of his favorites was asking, "What year is it," and pointing out that it was 2017 *AD*. Some people think of AD as "after death," but, according to *Merriam-Webster*, it actually stands for "*anno Domini*", Latin for "in the year of our Lord." In a YouTube video of his speech at the 2016 Western Conservative Summit (posted by the event's organizer, the Centennial Institute), Robertson asks the question: If Jesus isn't real, why do we count time by Him?

Natalie Burton posted a great video on YouTube of Phil's son Jase Robertson at a speaking engagement in Kansas. Jase tells the story of how, at age sixteen, he presented the gospel to his friends, who were in the middle of getting drunk at a football game. He posed three questions to them: How did you get to the earth? What are you supposed to be doing here? How are you leaving? Also in the video, he points out an awesome story in last chapter of John's gospel where the resurrected Jesus is part of a fishing party that catches 153 fish.

At the top of the video list for me, however, is Doctor Frank Turek. This award-winning author and public speaker does an incredible job as an apologist, going around to college campuses and discussing whether God is real. "Matty John 14:6" posted a video on YouTube in which Frank Turek asks his famous question: "If Christianity were true, would you become a Christian?"

Some people are so caught up in their sin that nothing you can do will change their minds. Others have been hurt and place so much of the blame on God that their eyes, ears and minds are closed. Other than that, though, how could you really answer, "No," if Christianity is true? In the video mentioned above, Turek presents four questions to answer to show that Christianity is indeed true.

The first question is: "Does truth exist?"

Many people today have adopted the approach of "You have your truth, and I have mine." Turek's response when people say that there is no truth or that all truth is relative is to ask them, "Is that true? Is it true that there is no truth? Because if it's true that there is no truth, the claim 'There is no truth' can't be true, but it claims to be true."

I look at this like *not* brushing your teeth. Maybe you can get away with it for years, but at some point, it is going to catch up to you. You are going to suffer some serious pain and probably lose your teeth if you don't take care of them. If God is true, you can probably live without him for a long time, but at some point, it is going to catch up with you, especially when your time here on Earth ends. Sometimes that end comes sooner than expected.

Turek's second question is: "Does God exist?"

Pascal's Wager (discussed in great detail by Paul Saka in his article for the Internet Encyclopedia of Philosophy) is a philosophical argument devised by the seventeenth century French philosopher, mathematician and physicist Blaise Pascal. As Paul Saka explains it:

> Pascal begins with a two-by-two matrix: either God exists or does not, and either you believe or do not. If God exists then theists will enjoy eternal bliss ... while atheists will suffer eternal damnation.... If God does not exist then theists will enjoy finite happiness before they die ... and atheists will enjoy finite happiness too, though not so much because they will experience angst

rather than the comforts of religion. Regardless of whether God exists, then, theists have it better than atheists; hence belief in God is the most rational belief to have.

In other words, a believer may reap infinite reward, while a disbeliever risks infinite loss. As Pascal put it:

> Now, what harm will befall you in taking this side [belief in God]? You will be faithful, humble, grateful, generous, a sincere friend, truthful. Certainly you will not have those poisonous pleasures, glory and luxury; but will you not have others? I will tell you that you will thereby gain in this life, and that, at each step you take on this road, you will see so great certainty of gain, so much nothingness in what you risk, that you will at last recognise that you have wagered for something certain and infinite, for which you have given nothing.

At your death, therefore, you are going to discover if God is real.

Turek spends time on the complexity of the human body and how that points to the existence of a Creator. He also talks about morality. If there were no moral law, he asks, why would it be wrong to torture a baby? It would just be your opinion versus the opinion of a baby torturer.

Next, Turek asks: "Are miracles possible?"

He points out that the greatest miracle in the Bible is creation. If God created the heavens and the earth, then every other miracle is certainly possible, including the resurrection. As Frank Turek points out, we now have evidence that is leading many scientists to suggest that the universe had a beginning out of nothing. "If that's the case, whatever created space, time and matter can't be made of space, time and matter, right? In other words, It must be spaceless, timeless, immaterial, powerful to create the universe out of nothing, personal in order to choose to create, also intelligent because the universe is also fine-tuned."

Finally, Turek asks: "Is the New Testament, and therefore the Bible, true?"

One of the really interesting things that he points out is the embarrassing details that are in the Bible. Jesus calls Peter Satan; don't you think Peter would have liked that left out? All four gospels point out that the women were the first to go to Jesus' tomb, while the men were locked up and scared. If the men were making up a story, do you really think they would have told it that way?

As Mark Humphries points out in *Early Christianity*, the Dead Sea scrolls "first came to public attention in 1947" and "were discovered quite by accident in a number of caves located near the remains of an ancient religious community at Qumran by the north-western shores of the Dead Sea." According to Humphries, they are "dated to the years between c. 225 BC and AD 70, with the majority belonging towards the end of that period." According to the Leon Levy Dead Sea Scrolls Digital Library published online by the Israel Antiquities Authority, "About 230 manuscripts are referred to as 'biblical Scrolls'. These are copies of works that are now part of the Hebrew Bible." One of them, now termed the Great Isaiah Scroll (1QIsa$^a$) according to the Israel Museum, Jerusalem, is of particular interest, as it contains "all 66 chapters of the Hebrew version of the biblical Book of Isaiah."

The book of Isaiah adds to the believability of the Bible, in that it is a miniature Bible. According to "Interesting Facts About Isaiah" by Donnie S. Barnes, Doctor of Theology, Isaiah was broken up into sixty-six chapters, just like the Bible has sixty-six books. There are thirty-nine books in the Old Testament, and the first thirty-nine chapters of Isaiah are similar in that they are "filled with judgment upon immoral and idolatrous men" (people). The final twenty-seven chapters "declare a message of hope," similar to the twenty-seven books of the New Testament.

Shari Abbott (in the article "Which Old Testament Book Did Jesus Quote Most Often?") cites eleven instances in the gospels in which Jesus refers to the book of Isaiah, though Shari does not mention the multiple instances in John 12.

I have come to understand that God allows us to go through tough situations, in order to build us up. We get stronger physically by lifting weights. We get stronger mentally and spiritually by lifting weights as well. There is Heaven. There is hell. There is Earth, with a little bit of both. God had me go through some hell in order to shape me.

I still struggle with my confidence. I hate that my poor choices hurt people. There are times that the devil convinces me that I am no good. He tells me that I just need to sit down and shut up about my Jesus. He paralyzes me with fear. The anxiety builds in my chest to the point that I can't breathe. I whine and complain and make excuses about why God didn't answer my prayers for wisdom.

As time heals some of the pain, however, I realize that God had a plan. He wanted me to go to the next level in my relationship with Him. He wants me to trust Him in the things that I can't fix and know that it's OK.

I don't fear what others might think of me as much as I used to because I have been through a situation where people didn't think much of me.

So where are you on your Christian walk? Do you have a personal relationship with Jesus Christ? Are you a lukewarm Christian? The God of the universe wants to have a relationship with you. How can you be lukewarm about that?

Faith is a big part of being a Christian, but when I look at all the evidence that I have presented here, I think it takes more faith to be an atheist.

*James W. Minton, Sr. (Jim)*

"I am not what I *ought* to be! Ah! how imperfect and deficient!--I am not what I *wish* to be! I 'abhor what is evil,' and I would 'cleave to what is good!'--I am not what I *hope* to be!--Soon, soon, I shall put off mortality: and with mortality all sin and imperfection! Yet, though I am not what I *ought* to be, nor what I *wish* to be, nor what I *hope* to be, I can truly say, I am not what I *once* was--a slave to sin and Satan; and I can heartily join with the Apostle, and acknowledge; *By the grace of God, I am what I am!*"

--John Newton
(author of the song "Amazing Grace" discussed in Principal #2)
Quoted in *The Christian Spectator: Volume III* (1821)

# Teachable Moments

1 Thessalonians 2:11-12 NIV: "For you know that we dealt with each of you as a father deals with his own children, encouraging, comforting and urging you to live lives worthy of God, who calls you into his kingdom and glory."

I remember when Gary Yuenger was teaching me to hit a golf ball. He said you have to hit the ball with the big muscles in your back. I couldn't figure it out. I wanted to throw my hands at the bottom of the swing, and that led to a lot of short shots that drifted to the right. Then I did it. I hit one just right. What he had been telling me now made sense. Back when I was playing a lot, I got down to a five handicap. I have had a lot of fun over the last fifteen years since I successfully learned how to hit a golf ball.

I wish I could tell you that parenting was easy and give you just that one perfect piece of advice. The fact of the matter is it is just like anything that is worthwhile: It requires hard work. There's a great quote from Robert Fulghum (quoted by Bonita Jean Zimmer in *Reflections for Tending the Sacred Garden*): "Don't worry that children never listen to you; worry that they are always watching you."

I have always told my kids to do as I say, not as I do, because I know I am a flawed human being. Jesus should be the standard to judge by, not me. In reality, though, a great deal of what kids learn is caught and not taught.

My goal was to set my kids' moral compasses in such a way that they knew the difference between right and wrong. I love the concept of the thirteen principles because these are simple little phrases that you can remember. If you can get this code of conduct ingrained in your kids' hearts, you can expect them to make better decisions down the road.

It is good to have rules, such as an 11:00 p.m. curfew, but I think it is more effective to help your kids learn why you want them home at the hour. Over the years, I have sent my kids many articles and videos of all the bad things that happen after 11:00 p.m., that most drunk driving occurs after this hour, for instance. It also starts you off running behind the next day. Most productive people are up and going early and not burning the candle at both ends.

Sometimes it is OK to say, "Because I said so." You are the authority, and your kids should respect that. That being said, I think it is best to develop a relationship with your kids where they understand that there are methods to your madness.

The big key is to take advantage of teachable moments! When your kids have questions, you need to be ready with a great response. You don't have to be able to answer every question, but you need to be able to help them work their way through the ups and downs of life. In this book, I hope I have been able to share with you what has worked for our family.

Kurtis and I talked occasionally about the "I love you, ifs." We should love our kids unconditionally. My parents were incredible at doing that for me. I have never been very good at it. I was often guilty of, "I love you, if you get an A," or, "I love you, if you get a hit." The way God wired me, I could make myself physically sick when Kurtis went 0-for-4 in a baseball game. That was something I needed to work on, and I still do.

In the introduction, I mentioned how I was with J. J. and my first go-around with parenting. Too often, I looked at J. J. as my child; I viewed him as an extension of myself and in relation to myself, rather than as an individual in his own right. It didn't help that his name was James Walter Minton, Jr. As a result, when J. J.

would do something wrong, I always felt like he was doing it to me. My mind would say, "Don't you realize what you are doing to my reputation?" In hindsight, I realize that I was doing a lot more than he was doing to hurt people's perceptions of me.

I did a great deal better with Kurtis and Emily, but I still struggled. We had a lot of fun with a John Wooden line (mentioned in his February 2001 TED Talk, for instance) that a C is only appropriate for the neighbor's children. Writing a book like this puts a great deal of expectations on the kids, but I think they are OK with it.

Try your best to love your kids not because of what they do but for who they are.

Remember Stevie Urkel on the TV show *Family Matters*? After he made a mess of things, he would say, "Did I do that?" Hopefully you can remember Urkel's whiny voice. When I turned fifty years old, Kurtis posted on Facebook:

> A big happy 50th birthday to the greatest dad a kid could ask for! Not only has he instilled in me a passion and love for baseball and the St. Louis Cardinals but also a passion and love for Jesus and sharing his love with others! Thanks dad for the countless number of things you have done for me and our family! I am the man I am today because of you. You're the greatest blessing in my life! Love ya and have a great day!

At another point, Suzanne posted a meme stating, "A daughter needs a dad to be the standard against which she will judge all other men," and captioned that with:

> So True! Made me stop this morning and thank God for the wonderful father my husband is to all of our children. It's what attracted me to him

some 27+ years ago! God has been faithful in blessing him greatly in the Dadittude area. Sure, he's often the "good cop" to my "bad cop" or the "gospel" to my "law," and often forgets to hang up his bath towel and knows all about spoilin--but he is a GREAT dad and Papa! Thanks Jim for leading our family and keeping us centered on Christ! Loving and appreciating you more each day!

Did I do that? Did I really go from not having a clue about how to be a dad to looking back and saying things turned out OK?

I think I failed forward.

Throughout this book, I have mentioned my shortcomings. It's not about how great we are; it's about how great God is. The One who designed the stars millions of miles away, the One who designed the smallest atoms from which all things are made, that same One is interested in the number of hairs you have on your head.

There is no way that I can live up to the thirteen principles in this book without God's help. Does God still do miracles? It is a miracle if a guy like me can get better at the stuff that I talk about in this book. I will never get to a ten on any sort of meter, scale or gauge, but I can improve.

People of the world will tell you that they can be moral without God. It's great that the liberals are trying to "out-nice" the Christians. There are always exceptions to the rule. As a general rule, however, the world at its worst needs the church and the family at their best.

To get society right, we need to get the church right.

To get the church right, we need to get the family right.

To get families right, we need to get marriages right.

To get marriages right, we need to get men right.

If we can all have our kids turn out better than we are, then we will build the home and change the world. It all starts with better dads.

# Bibliography

100huntley. "Running From Pain and Finding Hope – Pattie Mallette 1/4". Filmed [May 2010]. YouTube video, 8:31. Posted [May 2010]. https://www.youtube.com/watch?v= NWozCvf2H5E.

---. "Running From Pain and Finding Hope – Pattie Mallette 2/4". Filmed [May 2010]. YouTube video, 8:00. Posted [May 2010]. https://www.youtube.com/watch?v=p-cHkegGezc.

---. "Running From Pain and Finding Hope – Pattie Mallette 3/4". Filmed [May 2010]. YouTube video, 8:23. Posted [May 2010]. https://www.youtube.com/watch?v=dMp08SVsQnM.

---. "Running From Pain and Finding Hope – Pattie Mallette 4/4". Filmed [May 2010]. YouTube video, 3:01. Posted [May 2010]. https://www.youtube.com/watch?v=7EJw8ZrAlyU.

A&E Television Networks, LLC. "This Day in History: JUL 30: Presidential: 1956: President Eisenhower signs "In God We Trust" into law." History.com. https://www.history.com/this-day-in-history/president-eisenhower-signs-in-god-we-trust-into-law (accessed July 9, 2018).

Abbott, Shari. "Which Old Testament Book Did Jesus Quote Most Often?" Reasons for Hope* Jesus. https://reasonsforhopejesus.com/old-testament-book-jesus-quote-often/ (accessed September 11, 2018).

Above Inspiration. "Tim Tebow Tells Incredible Story of John 3:16". Filmed [September 2017]. YouTube video, 6:32. Posted

[September 2017]. https://www.youtube.com/watch?v= NPkz6Cd4xGU.

American Humanist Association. "Are You a Humanist?" AmericanHumanist.org. https://americanhumanist.org/ what-is-humanism/ (accessed July 6, 2018).

Andrews, Andy. "Baseball, Boys & Bad Words." Recorded March 19, 2002. Track 6 on *My Life So Far.* Scream Marketing, Compact disc.

*The Andy Griffith Show.* "Opie the Birdman." Directed by Dick [Richard] Crenna. Written by Harvey Bullock. CBS, September 30 1963.

---. "Opie and the Spoiled Kid." Directed by Bob Sweeney. Written by Jim Fritzell and Everett Greenbaum. CBS, February 18 1963.

Avalon. "Testify to Love." By Jody McBrayer, Michael Passons, Janna Long, and Nikki Hassman-Anders. Recorded 1997. Track 1 on *A Maze of Grace.* Sparrow, Compact disc.

B, Richie. "Marc Mero's Powerful Message About A Mothers Love". Filmed [May 2015]. YouTube video, 5:45. Posted [May 2015]. https://www.youtube.com/watch?v=3eFUP-Q0ui8.

Baldwin, James. *Nobody Knows My Name.* New York: Dial Press, 1961.

Barna Group. "Changes in Worldview Among Christians over the Past 13 Years." Barna.com. https://www.barna.com/ research/barna-survey-examines-changes-in-worldview-among-christians-over-the-past-13-years/ (accessed July 10, 2018).

Barnes, Donnie S. "Interesting Facts About Isaiah." BibleCharts.org. http://www.biblecharts.org/thebible/ interestingfactsaboutisaiah.pdf (accessed September 11, 2018).

TheBestSchools.org. "Interview with Dr. Ben Carson on Education." TheBestSchools.org. https://thebestschools.org/

magazine/ben-carson-interview-on-education/ (accessed August 16, 2018).

Betsch, Mara. "8 Simple Rules for Dating a Duggar Daughter." TLC.com. http://www.tlc.com/tv-shows/19-kids-and-counting/games-and-more/rules-dating-duggar-daughter/ (accessed August 20, 2018).

Beyond the Ultimate. "Matt Holliday." BeyondTheUltimate.org. http://www.beyondtheultimate.org/athlete/Matt-Holliday (accessed August 24, 2018).

The Bible Project. "The Bible Project." The Bible Project. https:// thebibleproject.com/ (accessed September 5, 2018).

Blanchard, Kenneth, and Spencer Johnson. *The One Minute Manager*. New York: William Morrow and Company, 1982.

Blume, Butch. "Baucham: Believing the Bible is a matter of reason." *The Courier*. https://baptistcourier.com/2015/02/baucham-believing-bible-matter-reason/ (accessed July 5, 2018).

Boley, Kevin. Twitter Post. January 5, 2014, 9:39 AM. https:// twitter.com/titanone/status/419885917466132480.

Bonhoeffer, Dietrich. *The Cost of Discipleship*. 1959. Translated by R.H. Fuller and Irmgard Booth. Reprint, New York: Touchstone, 1995.

Bossip. "God Flow: Christian Rapper Lecrae Talks Gospel & Culture In Hip Hop | 2016 BET Hip Hop Awards". Filmed [October 2016]. YouTube video, 1:48. Posted [October 2016]. https://www.youtube.com/watch?v=9boD03b0TPg.

Brooks, Phillips. "Easter Day." In *Sermons for the Principal Festivals and Fasts of the Church Year*. 1895. Edited by John Cotton Brooks. Seventh Series, New York: E.P. Dutton & Co., 1910.

Burke, John. *Imagine Heaven: Near-Death Experiences, God's Promises, and the Exhilarating Future That Awaits You*. Grand Rapids: Baker Books, 2015.

Burton, Natalie. "Jase Robertson - How'd you get to the Earth, Why are you here, How are you leavin'". Filmed [December 2012]. YouTube video, 4:43. Posted [December 2012]. https://www.youtube.com/watch?v=rpj7CyzxJN4.

Carey, Michelle. "The Butterfly Effect by Andy Andrews". Filmed [May 2008]. YouTube video, 9:45. Posted [June 2013]. https://www.youtube.com/watch?v=mo6fBAT8f-s.

Carver, George. "George Washington Carver National Monument: Carver Quotes." [Page 2]. National Park Service. 8 Jul 2009. Internet Archive. https://web.archive.org/web/20090708005845/http://www.nps.gov/archive/gwca/expanded/quotes_2.htm (accessed July 17, 2018).

Cathy, Dan T. "Leadership Toolkit: Side Towel". Filmed [July 2011]. YouTube video, 2:36. Posted [July 2011]. https://www.youtube.com/watch?v=ASi7fLUYLs8.

Centennial Institute. "Phil Robertson - Western Conservative Summit 2016". Filmed [July 2016]. YouTube video, 48:34. Posted [July 2016]. https://www.youtube.com/watch?v=TIq1XmnG4-U.

Centers for Disease Control and Prevention (CDC). "Life Expectancy." CDC.gov. https://www.cdc.gov/nchs/fastats/life-expectancy.htm (accessed August 21, 2018).

The Christian Spectator. "Anecdote of the Late Rev. John Newton." In *The Christian Spectator, Conducted By an Association of Gentlemen. For the Year 1821. Volume III.* New Haven: S. Converse, 1821.

Collins, Jim [James C.]. *Good to Great: Why Some Companies Make the Leap . . . And Others Don't.* New York: Harper Business, 2001.

Collins, Jim. *Uncommon Hope: One Team . . . One Town . . . One Tragedy . . . One Life-Changing Season.* Bloomington, IN: WestBow Press, 2016.

Covey, Stephen. *The 7 Habits of Highly Effective People.* New York: Free Press, 1989.

Davis, Scott. "Stephen Curry spent a summer in high school changing his shooting form to become the NBA's greatest shooter." *Business Insider.* https://www.businessinsider.com/stephen-curry-changed-shooting-form-nbas-greatest-shooter-2016-5 (accessed August 17, 2018).

DC Talk. "Jesus Freak." By Toby McKeehan and Mark Heimermann. Recorded 1995. Track 22 on *WOW #1s: 31 of the Greatest Christian Music Hits Ever.* Provident Music Distribution, Compact disc.

Denison, Jim. "What America Doesn't Understand about Tim Tebow." ChristianHeadlines.com. https://www.christianheadlines.com/columnists/denison-forum/what-america-doesn-t-understand-about-tim-tebow.html (accessed July 24, 2018).

Dennis, Hunter, Chuck Konzelman, and Cary Solomon. *God's Not Dead.* Directed by Harold Cronk. Los Angeles: Freestyle Releasing, 2014.

Dobson, John, and Shirley Dobson. *Night Light: A Devotional for Couples.* Sisters: Multnomah Publishers, 2000.

Drehs, Wayne. "SportsCenter: Featured: The Evolution of Michael Phelps". ESPN video, 15:01. 2016. http://www.espn.com/video/clip?id=17185805.

Drover. "City-Data Forum > U. S. Forums > Illinois > Decatur Illinois". City-Data.com. www.city-data.com/forum/illinois/30084-decatur-illinois.html. (accessed August 13, 2018).

Dungy, Tony. *Dare to Be Uncommon Men's Bible Study.* Loveland: Group Publishing, 2009.

*E:60.* "E:60 Heartland." Directed by Ben Houser. ESPN, April 13, 2010.

EBC. "Dabo Swinney - On Kaepernick - I hate to see what is going on in our country". Filmed [September 2016]. YouTube video, 10:34. Posted [September 2016]. https://www.youtube.com/watch?v=spxesk4-K8g&t=375s.

Engel, Pamela. "How Trump came up with his slogan 'Make America Great Again.'" BusinessInider.com. http://www. businessinsider.com/trump-make-america-great-again-slogan-history-2017-1 (accessed July 3, 2018).

Erwin, Jon, and Quinton Peeples based upon the book by Todd Gerelds and Mark Shlabach. *Woodlawn.* DVD. Directed by Andrew Erwin and Jon Erwin. Los Angeles: Universal Pictures Home Entertainment, 2016.

ESPN Player. "CFB: Clemson head coach Dabo Swinney reflects on his life". [Original title: "Dabo's Journey"]. Filmed [January 2012]. YouTube video, 5:00. Posted [January 2012]. https://www.youtube.com/watch?v=hyBTKhRtXp0.

FCA [Fellowship of Christian Athletes]. "Dabo Swinney Featured on FCA Magazine." FCA.org. https://www.fca.org/magazine-story/2017/09/14/dabo-swinney-featured-on-fca-magazine (accessed August 23, 2018).

FCA [Fellowship of Christian Athletes] Coaches Academy. "3Dimensional Coaching." PDF file. FCACoachesAcademy.com. http://fcacoachesacademy.com/Websites/fcacoachesacademy/images/101_handout.pdf (accessed July 20, 2018).

Florida Department of State. "State Motto." DoS.MyFlorida. com. http://dos.myflorida.com/florida-facts/florida-state-symbols/state-motto/ (accessed July 9, 2018).

Focus on the Family. "Pain, Injustice, and God's Love." FocusOnTheFamily.com. https://www.focusonthefamily.com/family-q-and-a/faith/pain-injustice-and-gods-love (accessed July 20, 2018).

Fulghum, Robert, quoted in Bonita Jean Zimmer. *Reflections for Tending the Sacred Garden: Embracing the Art of Slowing Down.* New York: iUniverse, Inc., 2003.

GaitherVEVO. "Bill & Gloria Gaither – Amazing Grace [Live]". Filmed [April 2012]. YouTube Video, 08:35. Posted [April 2012]. https://www.youtube.com/watch?v=qNuQbJst4Lk.

Gehrke, Robert. "During Utah fundraiser, Rice warns of 'entitlement' mentality." *The Salt Lake Tribune.* http://archive.sltrib.com/article.php?id=54850902&itype=CMSID (accessed August 6, 2018).

Gilmore, Jodie. "Man of science--and of God: George Washington Carver believed that Providence guided his scientific investigations and that those investigations led to a better understanding of God and His handiwork." *The New American,* January 26, 2004. Retrieved Jul 17 2018 from https://www.thefreelibrary.com/Man+of+science--and+of+God%3a+George+Washington+Carver+believed+that...-a0112794990.

Google Books. "The End of Stress: Four Steps to Rewire Your Brain." Google Books. https://books.google.com/books/about/The_End_of_Stress.html?id=EtOKBAAAQBAJ (accessed August 28, 2018).

Got Questions Ministries. "How to get to heaven - what are the ideas from the different religions?" GotQuestions.org. https://www.gotquestions.org/how-to-get-to-heaven.html (accessed August 21, 2018).

*The Haney Project.* "Michael Phelps: A New Beginning." Episode 1. Golf Channel, February 25, 2013.

Henry, Matthew. "Directions for Daily Communion with God, In Three Discourses, Showing How to Begin, How to Spend, and How to Close Every Day with God: The Third Discourse, Showing How to Close the Day with God." In *The Miscellaneous Works of the Rev. Matthew Henry, V.D.M., Containing in Addition to Those Heretofore Published Numerous Sermons, Now Printed from the Original Mss. An Appendix on What Christ Is Made to Believers, in Forty Real Benefits, by the Rev. Philip Henry, Never Before Published, Also a Preface and Life of the Rev. Matthew Henry, V.D.M., and Funeral Sermons on Mr. Matthew Henry by Tong, John Reynolds, and Dr. Williams.* London: Joseph Ogle Robinson, 1833.

Herman, Rhett. "How fast is the earth moving?" *Scientific American.* https://www.scientificamerican.com/article/ how-fast-is-the-earth-mov/ (accessed August 30, 2018).

Holtz, Lou. "Former coach Lou Holtz on anthem protests, NFL ratings". Filmed [September 2017]. Fox News video, 3:26. Posted [September 2017]. http://video.foxnews.com/ v/5594090453001/?#sp=show-clips.

Hoskins, Patricia. "Unashamed to rep God." BBC: Birmingham. http://www.bbc.co.uk/birmingham/content/articles/ 2008/08/07/unashamed_tour_birmingham_feature.shtml (accessed August 3, 2018).

Hughes, Patrick Henry. *s.n.* Motivational Speech, Community Leaders Breakfast, Decatur, IL, April 3, 2014.

Humphries, Mark. *Early Christianity.* New York: Routledge, 2006. http://dl4a.org/uploads/pdf/Early%20Christianity.pdf

Hunt, Josh. "Why We Must Discuss." JoshHunt.com. https:// www.joshhunt.com/2016/05/31/why-we-must-discuss-2/ (accessed July 30, 2018).

Hunter, Kent R. *Discover Your Windows.* Nashville: Abingdon Press, 2002.

Huntley, Walt. *Homespun Gospel: The Poetry of Walt Huntley.* Cooksville: Sunrise Productions, 1981.

IAmSecond.com. "Clayton Kershaw - White Chair Film - I Am Second®". Filmed [*n.d.*]. I Am Second video, 5:09. Posted [*n.d.*]. https://www.iamsecond.com/seconds/clayton-kershaw/.

---. "Lecrae - White Chair Film - I Am Second®". Filmed [*n.d.*]. I Am Second video, 9:09. Posted [*n.d.*]. https://www.iamsecond. com/seconds/lecrae/.

---. "Trevor Bayne - White Chair Film - I Am Second®". Filmed [*n.d.*]. I Am Second video, 6:25. Posted [*n.d.*]. https://www. iamsecond.com/seconds/trevor-bayne/.

Illinois High School Association. #MCstrong - UHIGH Baseball CoachMichaelCollinsLeavesLastingLegacy."IHSA.org.http:// www.ihsa.org/IHSAState/IHSAStateArticles/tabid/768/

articleType/ArticleView/articleId/408/MCstrong--UHIGH-Baseball-Coach-Michael-Collins-Leaves-Lasting-Legacy. aspx (accessed August 9, 2018).

Inabinett, Mark. "Tim Tebow wants his life - and yours--to have meaning beyond football (photos)." AL.com. https://www. al.com/sports/index.ssf/2013/04/tim_tebow_wants_his_ life_-_and.html (accessed July 25, 2018).

Internet Movie Database. "James Garner." IMDB.com. https:// www.imdb.com/name/nm0001258/bio?ref_=nm_ov_bio_ sm (accessed August 3, 2018).

Israel Antiquities Authority. "Introduction: Biblical Manuscripts." The Leon Levy Dead Sea Scrolls Digital Library. https://www. deadseascrolls.org.il/learn-about-the-scrolls/introduction (accessed September 11, 2018).

Israel Museum, Jerusalem. "The Great Isaiah Scroll." The Digital Dead Sea Scrolls. http://dss.collections.imj.org.il/isaiah (accessed September 11, 2018).

Jampolsky, Gerald G., MD. "About Jerry Jampolsky: About Jerry." Facebook. https://www.facebook.com/jerry.jampolsky (accessed August 28, 2018).

---. *Good-Bye to Guilt: Releasing Fear Through Forgiveness.* New York: Bantam Books, 1985.

---. *Love Is Letting Go of Fear.* Berkeley: Celestial Arts, 2004.

John Hopkins Medicine. "The Importance of Forgiveness". Filmed [May 2014]. YouTube video, 5:45. Posted [May 2014]. https:// www.youtube.com/watch?v=q8MQgyDomy0.

Johnson, Ken. *Journey to Excellence.* n.d. Helping Hands Group, Inc., Compact disc.

Johnson, Richard. "Clemson's national championship celebration was a religious revival." SBNation.com. https://www.sbnation. com/college-football/2017/1/14/14273814/clemson-national-championship-celebration-parade (accessed August 23, 2018).

Joseph, Andrew. "Kentucky fans trash ref Higgins' business on FB." *USA Today.* https://www.usatoday.com/story/sports/

ftw/2017/03/28/kentucky-fans-cross-the-line-by-trashing-referee-john-higgins-business-on-facebook/99747670/ (accessed August 21, 2018).

Kaufman, Fred, Jeremy Spear, and Juliet Weber. *Fastpitch.* Directed by Jeremy Spear and Juliet Weber. New York: Artistic License Films, 2000.

Kendrick, Alex, and Stephen Kendrick. *Courageous.* DVD. Directed by Alex Kendrick. Culver City: Sony Pictures Home Entertainment, 2012.

---. *Facing the Giants.* DVD. Directed by Alex Kendrick. Culver City: Sony Pictures Home Entertainment, 2007.

Kercheval, Ben. "Swinney misses mark with well-intentioned comments on Kaepernick protest." CBS Sports. https://www.cbssports.com/college-football/news/dabo-swinney-misses-the-mark-with-well-intentioned-comments-on-kaepernick-protest/ (accessed August 23, 2018).

King, Shaun. "KING: Clemson Coach Dabo Swinney's speech on injustice in America is the dumbest thing I've ever heard." *New York Daily News.* http://www.nydailynews.com/news/national/king-clemson-coach-swinney-speech-injustice-ridiculous-article-1.2792355 (accessed August 23, 2018).

Kinsella, W. P., and Phil Alden Robinson. *Field of Dreams.* Directed by Phil Alden Robinson. Universal City: Universal Pictures, 1989.

Knight, Steven. *Amazing Grace.* DVD. Directed by Michael Apted. Los Angeles: 20th Century Fox Home Entertainment, 2007.

Koren, Steve, Mark O'Keefe, and Steve Oedekerk. *Bruce Almighty.* Directed by Tom Shadyac. Universal City: Universal Pictures, 2003.

Korte, Lara. "Youth suicide rates are rising. School and the Internet may be to blame." *USA Today.* https://www.usatoday.com/story/news/nation-now/2017/05/30/youth-suicide-rates-rising-school-and-internet-may-blame/356539001/ (accessed July 20, 2018).

Krauss, Lawrence M. "Lawrence Krauss: From a Cosmic Perspective, We're Irrelevant. It's Up to Us to Give Our Lives Meaning.". Directed by Jonathan Fowler and Elizabeth Rodd. BigThink video, 1:55. 2017. https://bigthink.com/videos/lawrence-krauss-from-a-cosmic-perspective-were-irrelevant-its-up-to-us-to-give-our-lives-meaning.

Landers, Ann, quoted in Kevin Kruse. "Top 100 Inspirational Quotes." *Forbes.* https://www.forbes.com/sites/kevinkruse/2013/05/28/inspirational-quotes/2/#36cf75ce3ae9 (accessed July 3, 2018).

Lasseter, John, Pete Docter, Andrew Stanton, John Ranft, Joss Whedon, Joel Cohen, and Alec Sokolow. *Toy Story.* DVD. Directed by John Lasseter. Burbank: Walt Disney Home Entertainment, 2005.

Leman, Kevin. *Making Children Mind without Losing Yours.* Rev. ed. Grand Rapids: Revell, 2017.

Levy, Piet. "Skillet finds faith, strength in Wisconsin." *Post-Crescent.* https://www.postcrescent.com/story/entertainment/music/2016/08/27/skillet-finds-faith-strength-wisconsin/87724370/ (accessed August 2, 2018).

Lewis, C. S. "Christian Apologetics." Chap. 10 in *God in the Dock: Essays on Theology and Ethics.* Grand Rapids: William B. Eerdmans Publishing Co., 1970.

---. *The Weight of Glory.* 1949. Reprint, New York: Harper Collins, 2001.

Lindz. "The Truth Behind Clemson's Epic Win." Follow the Lindz. http://followthelindz.com/southern-charm/tiger-nation/ (accessed August 23, 2018).

Lucado, Max. *3:16: The Numbers of Hope.* Nashville: Thomas Nelson, 2007.

Luther, Martin. "The Small Catechism: Part 1: The Ten Commandments." Evangelical Lutheran Synod. http://els.org/beliefs/luthers-small-catechism/the-ten-commandments/ (accessed July 9, 2018).

MacArthur, John, Jr. *The Ultimate Priority: John MacArthur, Jr., on Worship*. Chicago: Moody Publishers, 1983.

Mail Foreign Service. "Life without limb-its: The amazing story of the man born without arms or legs . . . who plays golf, surfs, and swims." *Daily Mail*. *http://www.dailymail.co.uk/news/article-1196755/The-astonishing-story-man-born-arms-legs--world-famous-swimmer-surfer-footballer.html* (accessed August 7, 2018).

Mandisa. "Bleed the Same." Featuring TobyMac and Kirk Franklin. Recorded 2017. Track 6 on *Out of the Dark*. Sparrow, Compact disc.

---. "Overcomer." By David Garcia, Ben Glover, and Christopher Stevens. Recorded 2012-2013. Track 1 on *Overcomer*. Sparrow, Compact disc.

Matty John 14:6. "4 Questions that Show Christianity is True". Filmed [February 2017]. YouTube video, 27:48. Posted [February 2017]. https://www.youtube.com/watch?v= p3qtyzpaAgY.

Maxwell, John C. *Sometimes You Win--Sometimes You Learn*. New York: Center Street, 2013.

McBride, Tom, and Ron Nief. "The Mindset List of American Death and Remembrance: 1750-1800." Legacy.com. http://www.legacy.com/life-and-death/the-liberty-era.html (accessed August 21, 2018).

McDonald, Alexander Hugh. "Tacitus: Roman Historian." *Encyclopædia Britannica*. https://www.britannica.com/biography/Tacitus-Roman-historian (accessed September 6, 2018).

McDowell, Josh. "Rules without Relationships Lead to Rebellion | Building Relationships". Filmed [November 2010]. YouTube video, 02:27. Posted [November 2010]. https://www.youtube.com/watch?v=Tx1SOiawASw.

McKay, Cheryl, based upon the book by Jim Stovall. *The Ultimate Gift*. DVD. Directed by Michael O. Sajbel. Los Angeles: 20th Century Fox Home Entertainment, 2007.

Mero, Marc. "Welcome to Champion of Choices." ThinkPoz.org. https://thinkpoz.org/ (accessed July 30, 2018).

*Merriam-Webster, s.v.* "A.D.," accessed September 6, 2018, https://www.merriam-webster.com/dictionary/ad.

———. "worldview," accessed July 5, 2018, https://www.merriam-webster.com/dictionary/worldview.

Michael Jr. "[#15] A Time to Serve & A Time to Laugh | Break Time | Michael Jr.". Filmed [November 2015]. YouTube video, 9:11. Posted [November 2015]. https://www.youtube.com/watch?v=ydB-MOMcO-s.

Mickler, Lauren. "TWC News Austin: High School Blitz Interview with Apollos Hester". Filmed [September 2014]. YouTube video, 2:28. Posted [September 2014]. https://www.youtube.com/watch?v=X7ymriMhoj0.

Minton, Emily. *s.n.* Valedictorian Speech, Eighth Grade Graduation Ceremony from Lutheran School Association, Decatur, IL, June 1, 2011.

Minton, James W., Sr. *s.n.* Address, Hall of Fame Induction Ceremony from Illinois Amateur Softball Association, Decatur, IL, April 13, 2013.

Minton, Jim [James W., Sr.]. "The Road Ahead." *Herald & Review*, March 28, 2010.

Minton, Kurtis. *s.n.* Valedictorian Speech, Eighth Grade Graduation Ceremony from Lutheran School Association, Decatur, IL, May 28, 2010.

Molinero, Pablo J. Luis. "Chico y Chica." In *Morfogenia: Relatos para reflexionar*. Morrisville: Lulu Press, Inc., 2014.

Moore, Geoff. "Home Run." By Geoff Moore and the Distance. Recorded 1995. Track 1 on *Home Run!* ForeFront Records, Compact disc.

---. "New Americans." By Geoff Moore and the Distance. Recorded 1995. Track 2 on *Home Run!* ForeFront Records, Compact disc.

---. "Why Should the Devil (Have All the Good Music)." By Geoff Moore and the Distance. Recorded August 1993. Track 9 on *Evolution.* Capitol Christian Music Group, Compact disc.

Moore, Lecrae, and Jonathan Merritt. *Unashamed.* Nashville: B&H Publishing Group, 2016.

Mungai, Dave. "Choices". Filmed [March 2011]. YouTube video, 15:00. Posted [March 2011]. https://www.youtube.com/watch?v=4LLp80XVGd8&t=57s.

*NASCAR on Fox.* "Daytona 500." Season 11, Episode 3. Fox Broadcasting Company, February 20, 2011.

NASCARAllOut. "2011 Daytona 500". Filmed [March 2011]. YouTube video, 38:30. Posted [March 2011]. https://www.youtube.com/watch?v=tHWs8AhIBFw.

National Aeronautics and Space Administration (NASA). "Imagine the Universe: The Cosmic Distance Scale: The Nearest Star." National Aeronautics and Space Administration (NASA) Goddard Space Flight Center. https://imagine.gsfc.nasa.gov/features/cosmic/nearest_star_info.html (accessed August 30, 2018).

National Center for Education Statistics. "Fast Facts: Expenditures." NCES.ed.gov. https://nces.ed.gov/fastfacts/display.asp?id=66 (accessed August 15, 2018).

National Park Service. *Discovering George Washington Carver--A Man of Character.* Diamond: George Washington Carver National Monument. NPS.gov. https://www.nps.gov/gwca/learn/education/upload/Charactor%20Education%20Book%20Grade%202-3.pdf (accessed July 17, 2018).

---. "Sculptor Gutzon Borglum." National Park Service: Mount Rushmore: National Memorial South Dakota. https://www.nps.gov/moru/learn/historyculture/gutzon-borglum.htm (accessed August 31, 2018).

Nelson, Louis. "Sen. Tim Scott reveals incidents of being targeted by Capitol Police." *Politico.* https://www.politico.com/story/2016/07/tim-scott-capitol-racism-senate-225507 (accessed August 21, 2018).

NFL. "Tim Tebow Mic'd Up Leads Comeback vs. Bears (Week 14, 2011) | #MicdUpMondays | NFL". Filmed [December 11, 2011]. YouTube video, 6:16. Posted [May 30, 2016]. https://www.youtube.com/watch?v=Vmw7j6EN0x0.

Obama, Barack. "Remarks by the President on Economic Mobility." The White House: President Barack Obama. https://obamawhitehouse.archives.gov/the-press-office/2013/12/04/remarks-president-economic-mobility (accessed August 17, 2018).

Obsessive Hope. "Jen Ledger's Testimony". Filmed [January 2013]. YouTube video, 5:21. Posted [January 2013]. https://www.youtube.com/watch?v=fYS5PinCjps.

Oedekerk, Steve, Joel Cohen, and Alec Sokolow. *Evan Almighty.* DVD. Directed by Tom Shadyac. Universal City: Universal Pictures Home Entertainment, 2007.

Oklahoma City Thunder. "A Message of Strength, Faith and Love". Filmed [February 2016]. YouTube video, 7:26. Posted [February 2016]. https://www.youtube.com/watch?v=SXIz14VuQik&t=313s.

*Oprah's Lifeclass.* "Rick Warren: Winning the Hand You're Dealt." Oprah Winfrey Network (OWN), January 13, 2013.

OWN [Oprah Winfrey Network]. "Oprah's Forgiveness Aha! Moment | Oprah's Life Class | Oprah Winfrey Network". Filmed [October 2011]. YouTube video, 2:41. Posted [October 2011]. https://www.youtube.com/watch?v=Rwcp_oEIwnU.

*The O'Reilly Factor.* "June 3, 2011." Fox News Channel, June 3, 2011.

Pascal, Blaise. "On the Necessity of the Wager." Section III in *Pensées.* Translated by W. F. Trotter. New York: E. P. Dutton

& Co., 1958. http://www.gutenberg.org/files/18269/18269-h/18269-h.htm

Pawson, David. "Studying the Bible". Filmed [January 2016]. YouTube video, 1:29:40. Posted [January 2016]. https://www.youtube.com/watch?v=FX-mUmd_P4w&t=15s.

PBS (Public Broadcasting Service). "*Secrets of the Dead*: Unearthing History: The Great Fire of Rome: Background." PBS.org. http://www.pbs.org/wnet/secrets/great-fire-rome-background/1446/ (accessed September 6, 2018).

Pond, Dave. "Exhibit A." FCA.org. https://www.fca.org/magazine-story/2015/02/26/exhibit-a (accessed August 29, 2018).

Quinones, Julian, and Arijeta Lajka. "'What kind of society do you want to live in?': Inside the country where Down syndrome is disappearing." CBSNews.com. https://www.cbsnews.com/news/down-syndrome-iceland/ (accessed July 5, 2018).

R. B. "Ken Davis I'M NOT OKAY". Filmed [July 2017]. YouTube video, 53:10. Posted [July 2017]. https://www.youtube.com/watch?v=9V8RsPAzQNw.

*Real Time with Bill Maher*. s.n. Season 12, Episode 8. Directed by Paul Casey. Written by Scott Carter, T. Rafael Cimino, Adam Felber, Matt Gunn, Brian Jacobsmeyer, Jay Jaroch, Chris Kelly, Bill Maher, Billy Martin, and Danny Vermont. HBO, March 14, 2014.

Reeves, Jay. "Christian ministry sues watchdog group over hate label." *Chicago Tribune.* http://www.chicagotribune.com/news/sns-bc-us--ministry-splc-lawsuit-20170825-story.html (accessed July 9, 2018).

Renewed Strength Fitness. "Renewed Testimony - Michael Lorenzen". Filmed [January 2016]. YouTube video, 11:10. Posted [January 2016]. https://www.youtube.com/watch?v=dDQEzVs_4nY.

Reuters Staff. "Chicago homicides fall 16 percent in 2017." Reuters.com. https://www.reuters.com/article/us-crime-chicago/

chicago-homicides-fall-16-percent-in-2017-idUSKBN1EQ18F (accessed July 9, 2018).

Rhodes, Ron. *End-Times Super Trends: A Political, Economic, and Cultural Forecast of the Prophetic Future*. Eugene: Harvest House Publishers, 2017.

Rich, Mike. *The Rookie*. Directed by John Lee Hancock. Burbank: Buena Vista Pictures, 2002.

Riley, Jennifer. "Limbless Evangelist Preaches Joy In Christ." *Christian Post*. 30 Mar. 2008. 28 Jul. 2012. *Archive.Today*. https://archive.is/20120728122853/http://www.christianpost.com/Ministries/Figures/2008/03/limbless-evangelist-preaches-joy-in-christ-30/index.html.

Robbins, Anthony. *Power Talk! Rules: The Source of Pain and Pleasure*. Recorded 1993. Guthy|Renker, Audio cassettes.

Saka, Paul. "Pascal's Wager about God." Internet Encyclopedia of Philosophy. https://www.iep.utm.edu/pasc-wag/ (accessed September 7, 2018).

salemleader. "Patrick Henry Hughes -- I Believe". Filmed [April 2014]. YouTube video, 5:41. Posted [April 2014]. https://www.youtube.com/watch?v=jb7zjtvFzLI.

Savage, Jeff. *Tim Duncan*. Minneapolis: Lerner Publications Company, 2010.

Schultz, Mark. "He's My Son." Recorded 1999. Track 3 on *Mark Schultz*. Word Entertainment, Compact disc.

---. "I am the Way." Recorded 1999. Track 1 on *Mark Schultz*. Word Entertainment, Compact disc.

---. "Let's Go." Recorded 1999. Track 2 on *Mark Schultz*. Word Entertainment, Compact disc.

Scriven, Joseph M., and Charles C. Converse. "What a Friend We Have in Jesus." HymnTime.com. http://www.hymntime.com/tch/htm/w/a/f/wafwhij.htm (accessed July 6, 2018).

Sharp, Tim. "How Far is Earth from the Sun?" Space.com. https://www.space.com/17081-how-far-is-earth-from-the-sun.html (accessed August 30, 2018).

---. "How Far is the Moon?" Space.com. https://www.space.com/18145-how-far-is-the-moon.html (accessed August 30, 2018).

Shelton, Ron. *Bull Durham*. Directed by Ron Shelton. Los Angeles: Orion Pictures, 1988.

Skiena, Steven, and Charles B. Ward. "Who's Biggest? The 100 Most Significant Figures in History: A data-driven ranking. Plus, have former TIME people of the year been predictive?" *Time*. http://ideas.time.com/2013/12/10/whos-biggest-the-100-most-significant-figures-in-history/ (accessed July 5, 2018).

The Skit Guys. "Skit Guys - God's Chisel". Filmed [May 2010]. YouTube video, 9:15. Posted [May 2010]. https://www.youtube.com/watch?v=AhfUzodLRvk.

SlicedSmoke14. "2011 Daytona 500 - Trevor Bayne Victory Lane Interview". Filmed [February 2011]. YouTube video, 2:24. Posted [February 2011]. https://www.youtube.com/watch?v=S96-RjCs28Y.

Slim, Carlos, quoted in Joel Brown. "50 Powerful Carlos Slim Quotes to Motivate You." Addicted2Success.com. https://addicted2success.com/quotes/50-powerful-carlos-slim-quotes-to-motivate-you/ (accessed July 3, 2018).

Smedes, Lewis B. *The Art of Forgiving: When You Need to Forgive and Don't Know How*. 5th ed. New York: Ballantine Books, 1997.

Stanley, Andy. Twitter Post. April 17, 2013, 7:38 PM. https://twitter.com/AndyStanley/status/324713440541290498.

Steers, Edward, Jr. "You Can Fool All of the People Some of the Time...: Lincoln Never Said That." In *Myths, Hoaxes, and Confabulations Associated with Our Greatest President*. Lexington: The University Press of Kentucky, 2007.

Stonestreet, John, and Brett Kunkle. *A Practical Guide to Culture: Helping the Next Generation Navigate Today's World: 4-Chapter Sexuality Excerpt*. Colorado Springs: David C Cook, 2017. Kindle.

Stonestreet, John, and G. Shane Morris. "BreakPoint: Numbed by Videogames: Anesthetic for the Male Soul?" BreakPoint.org. http://www.breakpoint.org/2017/06/breakpoint-numbed-by-video-games/ (accessed July 25, 2018).

Superchick. "We Live." By Melissa Brock, Tricia Brock, Matt Dally, Dave Ghazarian, and Max Hsu. Recorded 2005. Track 10 on *Beauty from Pain*. Columbia, Compact disc.

Tacitus, Cornelius. "Book 15." In *The Annals of Tacitus: The translation of Alfred John Church and William Jackson Brodribb. With the etchings of Giovanni Battista Piranesi.* Philadephia: Franklin Books: 1st Edition, 1982. https://en.wikisource.org/wiki/The_Annals_(Tacitus)/Book_15.

Tarjanyi, Judy. "Columbine victim's dad traveling to share his daughter's journal." *Toledo Blade*, November 27, 2018. Accessed July 20, 2018. https://news.google.com/newspapers?nid=1350&dat=19991127&id=q8kwAAAAIBAJ&sjid=sAMEAAAAIBAJ&pg=2269,3922533&hl=en/.

Taylor, Thomas Rawson. "I'm But a Stranger Here." Hymnary. org. https://hymnary.org/text/im_but_a_stranger_here (accessed July 12, 2018).

Tebow, Tim. "Tim Tebow." TimTebow.com. https://www.timtebow.com/ (accessed July 24, 2018).

Tebow, Tim, and A. J. Gregory. *Shaken: Discovering Your True Identity in the Midst of Life's Storms.* New York: WaterBrook, 2016.

Tebow, Tim, and Nathan Whitaker. *Through My Eyes: A Quarterback's Journey.* New York: Harper Collins, 2011.

Tim Tebow Foundation. "Night to Shine." TimTebowFoundation. org. https://www.timtebowfoundation.org/ministries/night-to-shine (accessed March 10, 2017, and July 24, 2018).

TobyMac. "Lose My Soul." By Toby McKeehan. Recorded 2007. Track 13 on *Portable Sounds*. ForeFront Records, Compact disc.

Tuggle, Todd. "That One Thing- Rest". *That One Thing*. Podcast audio, June 4, 2017. http://renaissancedecatur.org/podcast/that-one-thing-week-2-todd-tuggle/.

The Veritas Forum. "What Makes Christianity Unique?". Filmed [December 2012]. YouTube video, 7:37. Posted [December 2012]. https://www.youtube.com/watch?v=DMc38L44avA&t=334s.

virtuousgirls1. "Jen Ledger: Drummer, Backing Vocalist for Skillet." The Virtuous Girls. https://virtuousgirls.wordpress.com/2014/08/05/jen-ledger-drummer-backing-vocalist-for-skillet/ (accessed August 2, 2018).

Visionary Family Ministries. "Rob & Amy Rienow: About Rob Rienow." VisionaryFam.com. http://visionaryfam.com/rienow/. (accessed August 13, 2018).

Vujicic, Nick. *Life Without Limits: Inspirations for a Ridiculously Good Life*. Colorado Springs: WaterBrook Press, 2012.

Wallace, Randall, Christopher Parker, Todd Burpo, and Lynn Vincent. *Heaven Is for Real*. DVD. Directed by Randall Wallace. Culver City: Sony Pictures Home Entertainment, 2014.

Warner, Anna B., and William B. Bradbury. "Jesus Loves Me." HymnTime.com. http://www.hymntime.com/tch/htm/j/e/s/u/jesuslme.htm (accessed July 6, 2018).

Warren, Rick. *40 Days of Purpose - Small Group Study Guide*. 3rd ed. Lake Forest, CA: Purpose Driven Ministries, 2003.

---. *The Purpose Driven Life: What on Earth Am I Here For?* Grand Rapids: Zondervan, 2002.

Watson, Benjamin, and Ken Petersen. *Under Our Skin: Getting Real About Race. Getting Free from the Fears and Frustrations That Divide Us*. Carol Stream: Tyndale Momentum, 2015.

Weisz, Claudia Minden. "And God Said No." Ephrata Ministries: The Heartbeat of the Remnant. http://www.ephrataministries.org/remnant-2011-07-God-said-no.a5w?A5W (accessed August 27, 2018).

Welland, Colin. *Chariots of Fire*. Directed by Hugh Hudson. Burbank: Warner Bros. Pictures, 1981.

West, Matthew. "Forgiveness." Recorded 2012. Track 3 on *Into the Light*. Sparrow, Compact disc.

---. "FORGIVENESS... Part 2 - THE REST OF THE STORY". Filmed [November 2012]. YouTube video, 5:26. Posted [November 2012]. https://www.youtube.com/watch?v=_18SzbjJgaE.

---. "Matthew West - Forgiveness (Live)". Filmed [August 2013]. YouTube video, 8:40. Posted [August 2013]. https://www.youtube.com/watch?v=n9J6xOT3Ldw.

Williams, H. K. "The Group Plan." *The Biblical World*, January 1919.

Winfrey, Oprah. "Thought for Today - Luck." Oprah.com. http://www.oprah.com/spirit/thought-for-today-luck (accessed August 14, 2018).

Wooden, John. "John Wooden | TED 2001 The difference between winning and losing". Filmed [February 2001]. TED Talk video, 17:31. Posted [February 2001]. https://www.ted.com/talks/john_wooden_on_the_difference_between_winning_and_success?language=en#t-446990.

Wooden, John, and Jay Carty. *Coach Wooden One-on-One: Inspiring Conversations on Purpose, Passion and the Pursuit of Success*. Grand Rapids: Revell, 2003.

Wooden, John, and Steve Jamison. *Coach Wooden's Leadership Game Plan for Success: 12 Lessons for Extraordinary Performance and Personal Excellence*. New York: McGraw-Hill, 2009.

---. *My Personal Best: Life Lessons from an All-American Journey*. New York: McGraw-Hill, 2004.

---. *The Wisdom of Wooden: My Century On and Off the Court*. New York: McGraw-Hill Education, 2010.

---. *Wooden: A Lifetime of Observations and Reflections On and Off the Court*. Lincolnwood: Contemporary Books, 1997.

Wooden, John, and Don Yaegeer. *A Gameplan for Life: The Power of Mentoring.* New York: Bloomsbury USA, 2009.

Yorkey, Mike. *Playing with Purpose: Tim Tebow.* Uhrichsville: Barbour Publishing, 2012.

Zobrist, Julianna. "Julianna Zobrist - Alive - Story Behind the Song". Filmed [November 2015]. YouTube video, 1:38. Posted [November 2015]. https://www.youtube.com/watch?v=9KBr_O54h0I.

Zobrist, Tom, and Bill Butterworth. *The Zobrist Family: Look What God Can Do.* Carol Stream: Tyndale House Publishers, 2018.

Printed in the United States
By Bookmasters